Drowning Girls in China

Drowning Girls in China

Female Infanticide since 1650

D. E. Mungello

ROWMAN & LITTLEFIELD PUBLISHERS, INC.
Lanham • Boulder • New York • Toronto • Plymouth, UK

ROWMAN & LITTLEFIELD PUBLISHERS, INC.

Published in the United States of America
by Rowman & Littlefield Publishers, Inc.
A wholly owned subsidiary of The Rowman & Littlefield Publishing Group, Inc.
4501 Forbes Boulevard, Suite 200, Lanham, Maryland 20706
www.rowmanlittlefield.com

Estover Road, Plymouth PL6 7PY, United Kingdom

British Library Cataloguing in Publication Information Available

Library of Congress Cataloging-in-Publication Data
Mungello, David E., 1943–
   Drowning girls in China : female infanticide since 1650 / D.E. Mungello.
      p. cm.
   Includes bibliographical references and index.
   ISBN-13: 978-0-7425-5530-3 (cloth : alk. paper)
   ISBN-10: 0-7425-5530-5 (cloth : alk. paper)
   ISBN-13: 978-0-7425-5531-0 (pbk. : alk. paper)
   ISBN-10: 0-7425-5531-3 (pbk. : alk. paper)
   e-ISBN-13: 978-0-7425-5732-1
   e-ISBN-10: 0-7425-5732-4
   1. Infanticide—China—History. I. Title.
   HV6541.C45M86 2008
   304.6′680951

                                                                    2008002614

Printed in the United States of America

∞™ The paper used in this publication meets the minimum requirements of
American National Standard for Information Sciences—Permanence of Paper
for Printed Library Materials, ANSI/NISO Z39.48-1992.

Contents

Illustrations

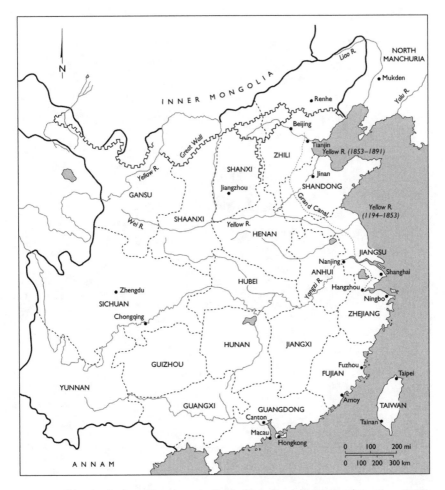

Map 1. China in the late Qing dynasty divided into its eighteen provinces (ca. 1878)

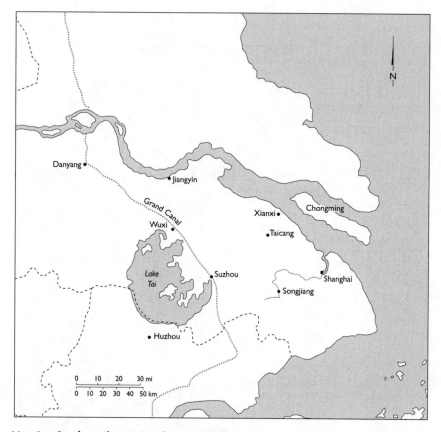

Map 2. Southern Jiangsu Province (ca. 1878)

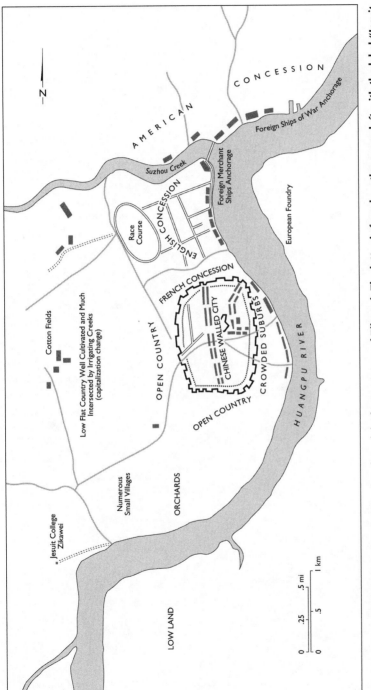
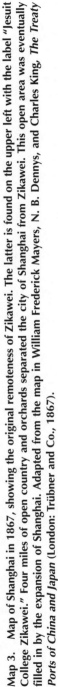

Map 3. Map of Shanghai in 1867, showing the original remoteness of Zikawei. The latter is found on the upper left with the label "Jesuit College Zikawei." Four miles of open country and orchards separated the city of Shanghai from Zikawei. This open area was eventually filled in by the expansion of Shanghai. Adapted from the map in William Frederick Mayers, N. B. Dennys, and Charles King, *The Treaty Ports of China and Japan* (London: Trübner and Co., 1867).

Preface

The killing of little girls in Chinese history presents a case of such helpless victims of atrocity that it cries out for identifying the culprits. But history, like people, is complicated. Female infanticide is one of the most controversial of historical topics. It is a topic that generates strong reactions from many sides and for many reasons. There is the sensitivity of the Chinese people with their long history of civilization. There is the political embarrassment and defensiveness of the Chinese government, whose restrictive birth-control policies since 1979 have revived female infanticide and the abandonment of girls. There are also the feelings of thousands of foreign parents who have adopted little girls from China.

My aim is to try to present the story of female infanticide in China, but I have been limited by the sources that I was able to find. Many people find the topic to be depressing, and it has not attracted much attention. The unequal distribution of sources on female infanticide that I was able to locate explains why I give more emphasis to the nineteenth century than to earlier centuries. Other sources from earlier periods probably exist and will be discovered by other researchers.

I have tried to understand the different ways people acted and to present their thinking as meaningful rather than merely irrational or cruel. Infanticide also involves issues that flow into the contemporary debate over abortion with its conflicting political, religious, and social perspectives. In fact, the Chinese historical justification of female infanticide bears certain parallels to the justification of present-day abortion in the Western world in terms of being a conflict of values. Although many of the specific values have changed, the nature of the conflict is similar. In earlier times in

China, the value of human life in its early stages competed with the lack of food and the family's desire for wealth, while today in the United States it competes with poverty and the rights of a woman to choose. If we can see the parallels between historical female infanticide in China and contemporary abortion in the United States, then we can view the Chinese in a deeper light. However, this is not a book of advocacy, and I would prefer to present it as a human rather than political story. If the moral issues cannot be avoided, I can, out of respect for all readers, try to describe them rather than preach them.

I confess at the outset my sympathy for the suffering of these little Chinese girls whose lives were cut short by infanticide in its various forms. To a lesser and more complicated extent, I sympathize with their mothers. The mothers' voices are rarely heard in all the documents produced by this controversy. The mothers were treated unfairly and were under unbearable pressure to produce boys rather than girls, but it is also true that the mothers were not completely powerless and were, more than anyone else, most directly responsible for killing their daughters. I have a daughter and a granddaughter and I can imagine how—in a different time and different place—their lives too might have been cut short at the point when they had barely begun.

I have attempted to convert all Chinese names and terms to pinyin romanization, which is the most standard in use today. When I was unable to identify the Chinese characters, I simply reproduced the romanization used in the nineteenth-century text. This nineteenth-century romanization is distinguished from pinyin romanization by the use of hyphens to divide syllables (characters).

A number of people have helped me write this book and I would like to acknowledge my debt to several of them. Professor Paul J. Bailey, Professor Henrietta Harrison, and Professor R. G. Tiedemann read early versions of the manuscript and offered helpful suggestions for improving it. Professor Cynthia J. Brokaw, Professor Jonathan Chaves, Dr. Claudia von Collani, Professor Robert E. Entenmann, Dr. Michelle King, Professor Kathleen Lodwick, Professor Susan L. Mann, Dr. Joanna Handlin Smith, and Julia Stone generously shared their knowledge and expertise. In addition, Professor Chaves kindly allowed me to reprint his translation of Jiang Shiquan's poem on infanticide. Dr. Ad Dudink helped me in numerous ways in locating and interpreting inaccessible documents. Professor Vincent Yang helped me with some Chinese translations. The Baylor University interlibrary loan staff provided me with indispensable assistance in securing books and documents from other libraries. Baylor University provided me with a research leave so that I could complete the manuscript. Susan McEachern of Rowman & Littlefield once again offered editorial support and skilled guidance. To all of these scholars and colleagues, I am deeply grateful. This book is dedicated to my recently born granddaughter, Madison Sue Pflum.

1

✢

Female Infanticide

INFANTICIDE IN WORLD HISTORY

In the Loess Plateau, a remote area of northern China along the Yellow River, the rural folk custom of afterlife marriage (*minghun*) lives on today.[1] In some villages, a son of at least twelve years of age who dies is eligible for a wife. The custom is part of traditional Chinese ancestral reverence, which believes that family members continue to exist in another realm after their death. For the sake of the dead person's happiness and to secure his blessing, living relatives attempt to find the deceased a wife, preferably a living woman. If a living woman is not available, they will sometimes buy a corpse. Families with daughters are willing to do this not only for the money. Traditional Chinese culture is a paternal clan culture in which a woman has a tenuous place in her family's genealogy and must marry in order to find a secure place in her husband's family tree. Families too poor to buy a minghun bride will make a straw figure and bury it beside their dead son as a wife.

The search for minghun wives is made more difficult by the scarcity of women in the Loess Plateau. The harsh conditions there cause young women to flee to the cities, where life is better. Another reason for the scarcity of women is a practice with a long history in China: the killing and abandonment of baby girls, generally referred to as female infanticide. In recent times, modern technology has enabled the killing of newborn girls to be replaced by sex-selective abortions, but the reasons for the abortions are similar to the reasons for the historical infanticides. The

1

causes of female infanticide have been both material and cultural, and they form the subject of this book.

Infanticide (child-murder) usually refers to the killing of newborn infants, although it has been applied in some contexts from the point of conception to two or three years of age. The most common methods involve drowning and exposure, but suffocation, starvation, strangulation, stabbing, poisoning, and burying alive are also used. In antiquity, infanticide was accepted as a practical expedient to deal with the ever-present danger of famine and starvation. From the beginning, more girls than boys were destroyed, probably as a form of birth control to reduce the number of potential mothers (and the number of mouths to feed), as well as for cultural reasons, such as eliminating the cost of a dowry.

Infanticide is not unique to China. Abandonment, infanticide, and abortion have been practiced in every society since antiquity, but with variations. The abandonment of infants has long captured the imagination of the world. Whether Moses or Romulus and Remus or Hou Ji, their abandonments enhanced their legendary paths to greatness. In the Middle East, Moses was found in a basket floating in the Nile River by the pharaoh's daughter, and he eventually led the enslaved Israelites to freedom. In Europe, Romulus and Remus were found on the banks of the Tiber River and suckled by a she-wolf, and then went on to found Rome. In China, the virgin Jiang Yuan conceived Hou Ji (Prince of Millet) after stepping on the footprint of God (*Shangdi*).[2] After she abandoned him as ill-omened, he was cared for by sheep and oxen, becoming known as Qi, the Abandoned.[3] She eventually took him back and he became the legendary progenitor of the Zhou dynastic line.

There have been many different ways of abandoning children, including selling them, placing them in institutions, and exposing them to the elements in public places. The ancient Greek philosophers Plato and Aristotle both recognized the benefits of exposure. The Hellenistic Greeks exposed mainly female infants, which produced a great discrepancy in the sex ratio of males to females. Exposure is often treated as synonymous with infanticide, on the assumption that the exposed child will inevitably die, but that is not always the case. In much of Europe, abandonment was a more benign alternative to infanticide.[4] In the late Roman Empire, most exposed children appear to have survived because the demand for laborers and servants had increased with the drying up of sources of slaves.

The emergence of Christianity in the late Roman Empire mitigated, but did not stop, the practice of abandoning children, even among Christians. Exposure was condemned as sinful if it amounted to infanticide, but not because parents had an obligation to support their children.[5] For these early Christians, parental attachment could become a form of worldly attachment and therefore undesirable. Abandonment was condemned if the child would die of hunger, be eaten by wild beasts, or possibly end up be-coming a prostitute who would unknowingly have incestuous relations with a parent. The concern of the early Christian church was to ensure that children were properly cared for, but not necessarily by their parents.

Throughout Europe in the Middle Ages there were numerous cases of "overlaying," or "overlying," in which the infant was said to be acciden-tally suffocated while sleeping in the parents' bed. The Renaissance artist Benvenuto Cellini (1500–1571) mentions in his famous autobiography that a woman caring for his young son had accidentally smothered him in this manner.[6] Many of these cases probably involved premeditated killing.[7] The situation in France was typical of Catholic Europe. In 1556 an edict of King Henri II equated infanticide with homicide, making it a cap-ital offense, while abandonment became a socially acceptable way of deal-ing with an unwanted child.[8]

Possibly as early as the fourteenth century in Rome, the first hospital *ruota* (turntable) was installed.[9] It enabled the mother to place her un-wanted (usually illegitimate) child on the turntable, ring a bell, and re-volve the turntable so that a nurse could receive the child on the other side of the wall without seeing the mother or asking any questions. In 1811 Napoleon decreed that each hospital should be equipped with a turntable (*tour*). Soon, more than one hundred thousand children a year were being abandoned on the *tours* of France. The numbers were so large that in France most of these turntables were dismantled by 1862. How-ever, their use continued extensively in Italy and other places.[10] In fact, such turntables are not merely a historical relic; they have recently been revived in countries trying to counter falling birthrates. Baby-drop (*Baby-klappe*) centers, which operate on the same principle as the turntables, were opened in Germany in 2000, and in 2007 plans were announced for opening one in Japan.

In the nineteenth century, China became an object of universal scorn for its widespread practice of infanticide, although the horror felt by Euro-peans was fed by a chauvinistic hypocrisy that blinded them to the mas-sive infant abandonments that were even then occurring across Europe.[11] Infant abandonment reached very high levels in eighteenth- and nineteenth-century Europe. However, the increase was greater in Catholic than in Protestant areas because Catholics made greater efforts to control illegiti-macy, driving unmarried mothers to abortion, infanticide, and abandon-ment.[12] Although there were far fewer abandonments in Protestant Eng-land, infanticide was nevertheless common in eighteenth- and nineteenth-century Britain.[13] By the mid-nineteenth century, lower-class parents were showing a great indifference to infant life. This led Parliament in 1872 to pass the first Infant Life Protection Act, which required all infants under one year of age to be registered and stillbirths to be reported.[14]

Catholic nations in Europe created large bureaucracies to administer the mass abandonment of infants. Consequently, the number of abandonments was greater in Catholic Italy, France, Spain, Portugal, Austria, and Belgium than in Protestant Prussia, England, Switzerland, and the United States. The eighteenth and nineteenth centuries witnessed the expansion of a state-run system for dealing with abandoned children. But what is notable is that the massive numbers of mostly illegitimate children handled by this system were evenly divided between boys and girls and not, as in China, predominantly female.[15]

INFANTICIDE IN CHINA

The prevalence of female infanticide in China can be traced to the low regard for girls that dated from Chinese antiquity. The *Book of Odes* (*Shijing*) is one of the oldest Chinese classics, dating from ca. 1000 BC to ca. 600 BC. It consists of 305 folk songs, hymns, and religious odes that Confucius supposedly selected from a larger collection of three thousand poems. Ode 189, which is believed to describe the building of the new capital of the Wei people in 658 BC, expresses this differing regard for boys and girls in the following verses.

> So he bears a son,
> And puts him to sleep upon a bed,
> Clothes him in robes,
> Gives him a jade scepter to play with.
> The child's howling is very lusty;
> In red greaves shall he flare,
> Be lord and king of house and home.
>
> Then he bears a daughter,
> And puts her upon the ground,
> Clothes her in swaddling-clothes,
> Gives her a loom-whorl to play with.
> For her no decorations, no emblems;
> Her only care, the wine and food,
> And how to give no trouble to father and mother.[16]

The different treatment of boys and girls reflected different expectations of what each one would cost and contribute to the family, and this attitude would later contribute to female infanticide. Concern over the abandonment of children was voiced as early as the Zhou dynasty (ca. 1050–256 BC). The Legalist statesman Guan Zhong (d. 645 BC), appointed guardians to see that orphans were provided for, and remitted taxes to those contributing to orphans' support.[17]

Female infanticide in China has a history of more than two thousand years. The earliest reference to it is found in a well-known passage from the *Han Feizi*, a work attributed to the philosopher Han Fei (ca. 280–233 BC).[18] Although prohibitions against child abandonment may be found in the Qin dynasty (255–206 BC) and Han dynasty (206 BC–AD 220) legal codes, it appears that transgressions were usually tolerated by officials and seldom punished. While the Legalist philosophy tended toward strict enforcement of the laws on infanticide and abandonment out of concern for cosmic order, Confucianism tended to be more concerned for human welfare. This concern for the well-being of the infants and parents led to a more tolerant application of the laws. Moreover, Confucians were more inclined to blame infant abandonment on the ruler's poor economic and political administration than on offending parents who lacked the material means to raise a child. Zhou dynasty philosophers, notably Mencius (fl. 350 BC) and Mozi, defended the people against condemnation for crimes committed out of poverty.

Although Han philosophers believed that human life had heavenly origins, the birth of individuals was not viewed as the product of a divine creator. Rather, birth and death were viewed more in Daoist terms in which birth represented a coming together of cosmic forces like *qi* (ether) while death represented the dispersion of these forces. While Christian morality regarded all human life as beginning at conception, the ancient Chinese delayed recognizing the newborn child's existence. This involved an ancient ritual in China by which a child's existence was not officially recognized until the third day after birth. "Not lifting up" (*buju* or *fuju*) a child within three days after birth referred to the rejection of a newborn by leaving it unattended with the intention of letting it die. The importance of this transition point is reinforced by the traditional Chinese rite of the third-day bath (*xisan*).[19]

The Confucian classic *Book of Rites* (*Liji*) describes the naming ceremony that occurred three months after the child's birth.[20] Part of the ceremony involved shaving off the child's hair, leaving only hornlike tufts on a boy and a circle on the crown of a girl. The *Book of Rites* refers only to a son, not a daughter, being carried by the mother to the father, who then named him. Much later, Qing dynasty (1644–1911) medical texts spoke of the third-day bath and first shaving of the baby's head as aimed at eradicating fetal pollution, and they reinforced the Chinese perspective that saw the newborn infant as emerging only gradually from a vegetative state of infancy (*yinger*).[21] However, this medical viewpoint was not entirely in harmony with Qing morality. It represented an earlier Daoist perspective that differed from Buddhism, which entered China in the first century AD. Buddhist reincarnation emphasized the continuity of the transmigration of a sentient being from one state of being to another, based on one's individual karma. Whereas the Daoist perspective tended to distinguish infanticide from murder on the grounds that the infant was not yet a fully developed human being, the Buddhists tended to condemn both acts equally. These conflicting viewpoints were synthesized in the popular moral teachings of the Qing, which blended the Three Teachings of Confucianism, Buddhism, and Daoism into one teaching.

It is not clear whether newborns were actively killed by drowning and other means in the Qin and Han dynasties, as they would be in later periods. Qin laws tried to treat abandonment and the active killing of a child as the same act. Parents found guilty of killing their children were to be tattooed and sentenced to penal servitude—the men as "wall builders" (*chengdan*) and the women as "grain pounders" (*chong*). Those guilty of killing someone else's child were to be subjected to the death sentence. However, the Han records contain few cases of officials punishing people for abandoning or killing infants, indicating that the laws on infanticide were rarely enforced.

A thousand years after the Han, the active killing of infants was well established in China. When the Song dynasty scholar-poet Su Shi, also known as Su Dongbo, retired in 1080 from official service to Huangzhou on the Yangzi River in Hubei Province, he heard that infant girls were being drowned in that region. He became so upset that that he was unable to eat, and he felt moved to write a letter of complaint to the local magistrate, expressing his concern in the following words:

> Poor farmers as a rule raise only two sons and one daughter, and kill babies at birth beyond this number. They especially dislike to raise daughters, with the result that there are more men than women and many bachelors in the country. A baby is often killed at birth by drowning in cold water, but in order to do this the baby's parents have to close their eyes and avert their faces while pressing the baby down in the water until it dies after crying a short moment.[22]

There were numerous reports of infanticide in Fujian Province during the Song dynasty. The scholar-official Wang Dechen (*jinshi* degree 1059) noted that if people in Fujian had more than three sons and two daughters, they would drown them.[23] Song literati ignored the evidence that infanticide was practiced by their peers and instead regarded it as a problem of the uneducated due to ignorance, selfishness, and evil. A few local officials in Fujian, such as Yu Wei and Zhu Song (1097–1143), tried to discourage the practice, but they met with limited results.

In the late Song, many poor families resorted to infanticide. In Fujian Province, the practice of "bathing the infant" (drowning the newborn infant in a bucket of water) was already prevalent but confined to rural districts.[24] In urban areas like Hangzhou, children were more likely to be exposed in the streets. In 1138, the Song court prohibited the practice and established orphanages. The earliest known case of a foundling hospice dated from 1247 and was called the Bureau of Childhood Mercy (*Ciyou ju*).[25] Marco Polo claimed that during the Yuan period (1279–1368) of Mongol conquest, Kublai Khan supported twenty thousand abandoned children each year through hiring wet nurses and providing orphanages. However, as is often the case with Marco Polo, there is little Chinese documentation to support his claim.

In the Ming period (1368–1644), Chinese continued to dispose of unwanted children by the traditional means of drowning them at birth or abandoning them to Buddhist monasteries. But the Qing period saw innovative attempts to fight infanticide led by local elites, who formed benevolent associations to establish foundling asylums and give direct aid (money, rice, and clothing) to the poor to assist them in raising rather than abandoning their children.

A SUBJECT OR A SENSIBILITY?

When European missionaries began arriving in China in 1579, they brought with them a set of feelings, or sensibility, that caused them to view female infanticide in a different light than the Chinese did. This sensibility was shaped by a Christian culture in which the Christ child was an object of reverence. The spiritual aura of the Christ child was transferred to all newborn infants in such a way that the sanctity of life was revered not in the venerability of old age, as was done in the Chinese style through filial piety, but in birth and infancy. The incarnation of God on earth in the Christ child was not only an idea or theological doctrine, but also a crucial part of this sensibility. Shaped by thousands of images of the Madonna and child, infanticide inspired horror in European (and particularly Catholic) eyes when it was encountered in China.

The pioneering Jesuit missionary Matteo Ricci, who lived in China from 1582 until his death in 1610, recorded in his journals that female infanticide occurred in several provinces of China.[26] It was caused by poverty, but he noted that it was rendered less barbaric by the widespread belief in Buddhist transmigration, which enabled the child to be reborn into a better life. The earliest reference to Christians baptizing abandoned children in China dates to 1612 in Nanjing.[27] In 1622 Fr. Pierre Van Spiere (de Spira) divided the Nanjing Christians into eight congregations and assigned them to perform works of mercy that included baptizing abandoned children. In Fujian in 1633 the Dominican Juan de Morales baptized moribund (dying) infants whose parents had abandoned them because of poverty and thrown them into the trash or rivers. (Dying children are said to be baptized *in articulo mortis*.) Later in the seventeenth century, the Christian literatus (Thomas) Li Jiugong of Fujian (d. 1681) condemned the drowning of girls in his book *Shensi lu* (Record of careful reflections).[28]

In 1634 a terrible famine struck Shanxi Province, causing the people to abandon their infants in large numbers. Two Jesuits based at Jiangzhou attempted to find and baptize these children. From dawn until dusk, the French priest Étienne Faber scoured the streets of Jiangzhou while the twenty-six-year-old Jesuit brother Manuel Gomez (Lu Youjiluo) searched around the walls surrounding the city.[29] Gomez was a Macauist, which meant that he was born in the Portuguese colony of Macau in southern China. Like many Macauists, he was the child of a mixed marriage: his father was a Malay from the Sunda Islands (present-day Indonesia) and his mother was Chinese.

Missionary accounts are filled with a certain type of story that was very moving to readers of that time. One of these stories tells how Gomez found an infant whose body was covered with vermin and had an open suppurating wound on the top of its head. Lacking enough holy water, Gomez approached a woman carrying a container of water and asked for a drink. He held the water in his mouth and quickly returned to the dying infant, spat the water into the hollow of his hand, and used it to baptize the child. After he pronounced the words of baptism, the child opened its eyes briefly and then closed them and died. Whereas we tend to see a story like this as morbid, its effusive emotionalism appealed to the baroque sensibility of Europeans of that age.

2

✝

Female Infanticide in Nineteenth-Century China

CAUSES AND FORMS OF INFANTICIDE

The term most commonly used in late Qing texts to refer to infanticide was *ni nü* (to drown girls), indicating that drowning was the prevalent method and girls were the primary victims. The term *ni nan* (to drown boys) was used far less often. The most common method involved plunging the infant headfirst into a large pot filled with water and holding her head underwater until she died by suffocation (*yansi zai shui pen*). Another method of infanticide involved suffocation either by pushing the infant's head into a container of ashes or by placing a piece of paper soaked in vinegar over the infant's face, cutting off air to the mouth and nostrils. The soaked-paper technique was found in the Canton region and was also said to have been used as a form of euthanasia for elderly and very ill persons who were in great discomfort.[1] Yet another method of infanticide involved crushing (*yansi ren*). The term *bi nü* (to kill a girl) was more general and sometimes used to refer to killing a girl through starvation.

Like drowning, the exposure of infants was a morally condemned and illegal act in China. As a result, exposure appears to have been practiced more in urban areas like Beijing where the safety of anonymity was more easily obtained. In rural areas and villages where most of the people lived and where anonymity was less possible, infanticide was more commonly practiced in the privacy of homes, where infants were killed soon after birth and passed off as stillbirths. Because most infanticides were hidden from observers, when European missionaries to China first discovered infanticide, they saw only the exposure of infants in public areas. This misleading impression was conveyed to Europe. Even in the nineteenth century, many foreign observers claimed that the relatively infrequent evidence of publicly exposed infants was proof that the Catholic missionaries were exaggerating the incidence of infanticide.

The most dramatic claim associated with public exposure was that exposed infants were sometimes eaten by wandering dogs and pigs. The shocking nature of this claim aroused skepticism among many foreigners. The less dramatic truth was that more mundane forms of abandonment were usually practiced. This involved placing the infant in a coarse basket (*lantun*) used for collecting manure and elevating it above the reach of dogs and pigs by wedging it into a tree, or suspending the basket from a tree or nailing it high up on a wall. The parents eased their consciences by hoping that someone would rescue and raise the child. Buddhist nunneries also provided small stone baby towers for depositing infants, although it is unclear whether the children placed in these towers were being exposed and offered up for adoption or were already dead and being placed in the towers for burial.[2] A missionary in Jiangxi Province wrote in 1845 that these abandoned infants often lived two days and nights, dying of hunger, cold, and heat while passersby ignored them.[3] Until its destruction in 1864, a well-known small circular baby tower stood near the road from the French Settlement in Shanghai to Zikawei.[4] Corpses of children were deposited there by parents too poor or unwilling to pay for burial.

Why were girls drowned in China? Sometimes they were killed for the same reasons as boys—because they were deformed or because they were born under unlucky astrological signs that might bring misfortune to the family. However, the primary reasons were economic and cultural. The economic reason involved severe poverty and the inability to feed the child. This factor caused the incidence of infanticide to ebb and flow, decreasing in good times and increasing in times of hardship, such as the 1634 famine in Shanxi Province or the Taiping Rebellion of 1850–1864. This fluctuation may have contributed to the ongoing controversy over the extent of infanticide in China. Clearly, the incidence of infanticide varied by time and region.

Another reason for female infanticide was cultural and involved the high cost of dowries. There was a telling phrase in Chinese that referred to daughters as "goods on which money is lost" (*pei jianhuo*). But this reason was also subject to fluctuations. When the number of females was reduced through infanticide or neglect, the sex ratios became imbalanced and the law of supply and demand made them more valuable. Because of this, in the eighteenth century, the marriage market for brides was a seller's one, with the result that "hypergamy" (marrying up) was as common as "matching doors" (a marriage between a couple of roughly comparable social background).[5] However, the demand for wives varied by region and period.

The idealized and most typical marriages in China involved a daughter who was raised in her family of birth until puberty and then sent into an arranged marriage, with her dowry being given to her husband's family. This type of marriage tended to be difficult for the young bride. She was cut off from her natal family, expected to perform menial duties, and supervised (and often tyrannized) by her mother-in-law. The key to improving her status lay in producing sons: through the obligations of filial piety, she could command a considerable degree of authority over them.

These women who were "espoused by betrothal" (*pin ze wei qi*) belonged to a select category of women who distinguished themselves from concubines and courtesans.[6] Whereas dowries in the Song dynasty (960–1279) had been an upper-class concern, by the Qing dynasty (1644–1911) they had become the mark of a respectable marriage. Households delayed marriages and went into debt in order to dower their daughters suitably. A dowry that matched or exceeded betrothal gifts and wedding costs paid by the groom's family confirmed that the bride was not being sold and so could enter married life with a respected status.

Although betrothed "major" marriages were the most idealized in China, there were other forms of marriage, albeit less desirable.[7] The absence of sons in a family might lead the family to negotiate an uxorilocal marriage in which a new son-in-law would come to live with them, instead of having their daughter marry and go to live with his family. Even less desirable were "minor" marriages, in which a family would adopt a girl at an early age with the intention of raising that girl to be a future wife for a son in the family. These girls were called *tongyangxi* (daughter-in-law raised from childhood).[8]

Minor marriages were quite common in certain areas of China—more so in the south than in the north—and they held practical advantages that saved many girls from being drowned or abandoned. Poor natal families unable to provide a dowry for a daughter often obtained payment in the form of a purchase price from the family adopting the girl. Although males exercised formal authority in family matters, in practice most decisions involving marriage were made by women.[9] Minor marriages, in particular, appear to have been a female strategy that suited the mother-in-law's purposes. There were also less desirable variations on this arrangement. Some girls were purchased at birth as servant-slaves although their owners frequently arranged marriages for them with an outsider when they reached marriageable age. Even less desirable was the purchase of very young girls for eventual prostitution.[10]

China has traditionally been a paternal-class culture in which a daughter had a very obscure place in her parents' family lineage. She was forced to leave her family to marry and have children in order to find a place within her husband's lineage. Males, not females, performed the family rites and ancestral ceremonies. In the eighteenth century, marriages were arranged by parents and took place when the woman was seventeen or eighteen years old and the man was twenty-one years old.[11] Although almost all women (but not all men) married, there was some female resistance to marriage in China. In addition to religious communities of celibate Buddhist nuns and laywomen, there were groups of Christian Virgins. There were also pockets of regional resistance to marriage. In the Canton delta in the late nineteenth century, some women refused to marry and took formal vows of spinsterhood.[12]

Marriages were arranged to encourage high birthrates. The demand for children was caused by the religious need for sons to maintain the patrilineal line. The demand was further increased by the high rate of infant mortality caused by diseases like tuberculosis and smallpox. Yet in spite of the demand for children, the fertility rates were low (5.5 children per woman) for that period in history. These low fertility rates have puzzled demographers and are probably explained by unrecorded births due to infant mortality and infanticide.

Members of Chinese families were stratified on the basis of age and sex, which was codified by law. Being older or male brought more elaborate ancestral rites than being younger or female.[13] Family members who died before the age of twelve and who were unmarried received minimal rites and had no spirit tablet in the family altar. One's status in ancestral worship depended on the all-important contribution to the family's organization and perpetuation. Given this perspective, newborn infants, especially girls, had the least value and were the most dispensable group. Since newborn females had lesser membership in their parents' family than did newborn males, their more transient status made them more vulnerable to infanticide.

Nevertheless, female infanticide was sometimes opposed because it impeded the generation of enough members to maintain a family line. Since the Song dynasty (960–1279), affluent families had been compiling family registers of their clans called *jiapu* or *zongpu*. These consisted mainly of genealogical tables with information about a lineage involving male agnatic descendants of a single ancestor along with their unmarried sisters and wives.[14] The family register of the Gu family of Haimen condemns the practice of killing the family's little girls.[15] Drawing on the fundamental elements of yang and yin (the complementary male and female forces in nature), the Gu family register speaks of the need to have both men and women in the perpetuation of the human race and to avoid destroying little girls by drowning. The register warns that those who commit such heinous crimes will be punished in the course of their reincarnation.

In the nineteenth century, female infanticide was practiced in most of the eighteen provinces of China. In the most thorough foreign study of female infanticide in China up to that time (1878), Fr. Gabriel Palatre collected documents from thirteen provinces while the *Annales de la Sainte-Enfance* (Annals of the Holy Childhood) documented infanticide in two more provinces (Shanxi and Sichuan). The documentation that Palatre collected indicates that infanticide was most pervasive in the Lower Yangzi River region and southeastern provinces of China. Research by contemporary Chinese scholars has confirmed that infanticide was more prevalent in the area of the Lower Yangzi.[16]

Dramatic stories of abandoned children were retold in Europe, where they evoked horror and sympathy. One of these stories was told by a Chinese seminarian in Macau about his origins in Shanxi Province:

> I was born in 1815. One month after my birth, my mother's milk quickly dried up, and my father, already provided for with two children who assured him against the cruel fate of dying without posterity, refused to find a wet nurse for me, although his wealth permitted it. In order to rid the family of me, he threw me into a muddy canal, located outside of a market town and near a large road. This conduct of my father ought not to be surprising, because it is common to all the pagans of my province. In Shanxi not only poor people, but even wealthy families, drown their children when their number exceeds two or three. There is an exception in this regard among the richest of my compatriots. The lot of young girls is even more to be pitied. You can judge by the following example: I have known a man who had suffocated seven out of nine that God had given him.
>
> A few moments after I had been thrown into this canal which would be my tomb, a traveler passed by; he heard my wails, descended from his camel, and seeing a child struggling in the mud, he retrieved me from being half-dead and carried me to a neighboring village.[17]

Although the notoriety of these abandonments of infants attracted attention in Europe, critics of the Catholic missionaries were correct in concluding that the relatively small number of observed infant abandonments could not account for the large number of infanticides claimed by groups like the Society of the Holy Childhood. Palatre addressed this contradiction on the very first page of his book. He pointed out that most cases of infanticide in China did not occur through exposure, but rather in the manner described in the Chinese documents and illustrated in the Chinese engravings reproduced in his book, namely, by drowning in the privacy of homes.

BUDDHISM AND DAOISM IN
POPULAR MORALITY LITERATURE

One of Palatre's most important sources of documentary evidence involved Chinese popular literature illustrated with engraved scenes depicting infanticide. These popular stories about infanticide are a mixture of history and folktales. They often include the names of people and historical towns, and even the dates of events. They appear to be based on actual incidents that over time were embellished by supernatural features, perhaps through oral traditions, before being transferred to written form. As pictorial art, the illustrations reproduced in Palatre's work are frequently stiff and graceless. They belong to a far less sophisticated art form than the famous Chinese landscape paintings being produced by literati artists. But unlike the landscape paintings, their purpose was didactic, not aesthetic. They were created to teach moral lessons.

Certain features (a pot, the king of hell, and the god of literature) are repeated in the illustrations to the point that they became part of an iconography of popular culture. Most of the illustrations contain the ominous symbol of a ceramic pot or wooden bucket filled with water. Sometimes the illustrations show the infant's feet sticking out of the pot. The presence of the pot conveyed that infanticide was either intended or had already occurred. The presence of the king of hell, Yanlou, conveyed the punishment in hell that was believed to be imposed on those who killed or assisted in killing daughters. The presence of the god of literature, Wenchang, symbolized the examination success that was said to be rewarded to those who saved little girls.

The main body of popular documents consisted of morality books (*shan shu*). This type of book originated in the Song period, but became much more widespread in the Yuan and Ming periods.[18] By the late Ming, they were being read by several strata of society, including the poor, the wealthy, and even scholars. The content of these works was a syncretic mixture of Confucianism, Daoism, and Buddhism. This was the realm of popular culture in which the reasoning was more practical than theoretical. Many of the stories were frightening, with the aim being to warn of the terrible consequences for those who drowned girls. These morality books emphasized that each person could control his or her fate by doing good deeds and avoiding bad deeds. In this perspective, there was a strong influence of Buddhist karma, which referred to the consequences of one's deeds. These consequences were believed to occur either in this life or in consequent lives through reincarnation. There was an emphasis on dispensing fitting rewards and punishments in terms of retributive justice (an eye for an eye, a tooth for a tooth).

While karmic fate involves retributive justice, there is also a tradition of compassion in Buddhism epitomized by the figure of the bodhisattva. A bodhisattva is someone who, while on the verge of attaining enlightenment, delays entry into the state of nirvana in order to assist others in achieving enlightenment.[19] This characteristic of charitable self-sacrifice distinguishes Mahayana Buddhism from the spiritual individualism of Hinayana Buddhism. The female Guanyin, who originated in India in the male form of Avalokitesvara, became the most well-known bodhisattva in China. *The Lotus Sutra* states that a woman who wants children, particularly sons, should pray to the Bodhisattva of Mercy, Guanyin, for assistance.[20] Guanyin is frequently portrayed holding a child and was often confused with the Madonna of Christianity. Consequently, it is not surprising that Guanyin is cited in one of the morality books as opposing female infanticide.[21] Ho-tong-tse (?) wrote that Guanyin opposed the drowning of girls on the grounds that both males and females were needed for procreation. Furthermore, she said that because of the law of karma, the drowned girl would return as a reincarnation to inflict retribution on those who drowned her. This manifestation of karmic justice was portrayed repeatedly in the morality stories.

The morality books confirm that the most common form of infanticide involved plunging the newborn headfirst into a container filled with enough water to drown her. This act was most commonly committed by the mother or midwife in the birthing chamber immediately after birth. A less common form of infanticide involved throwing the newborn into a lake or river; this might be done by the father.

The malnourishment of girls was a more passive form of infanticide. This could range from outright starvation to underfeeding or perhaps being prematurely weaned from breast-feeding, making the girl more vulnerable to illness and death. Boys tended to be better fed than girls in China and this partially accounts for the gender differences in infant mortality. The morality book *Guobao tu* (Just rewards illustrated) tells of a karmic debt paid by a tribunal secretary in Suzhou named He Yingyuan. He had one boy and one girl, followed by four more girls who he allowed to starve.[22] He was punished when his only son Shen was inflicted by demons with a serious illness. In spite of He Yingyuan's exhausting his savings in order to save his son, the boy died (see fig. 2.1). Since the boy died before he could be married, his father was left without posterity.

Suffocation in the ashes of a dustbin was a less common form of infanticide. In Jiangyin (in southern Jiangsu Province), a woman, Hu, is said to have suffocated two girls in the ashes of her hearth.[23] Later, in 1832, when she was at the full term of her pregnancy with another child, she suffered in labor for three days and her family prayed for her deliverance. Suddenly

戮女絕嗣

Figure 2.1. After He Yingyuan allowed four daughters (portrayed on his son's deathbed as demonic reincarnations) to starve, he was punished in karmic retribution by having his only son fall ill and die, leaving him without posterity. *Guobao tu*, one of four volumes that compose *Zhuyu yuan* (Shanghai, undated), p. 9, reproduced in Palatre, *L'infanticide*, p. 75 & appendix 34.

a girl's voice from her womb spoke, saying she was afraid to be born for fear of being disposed of in the dustbin like her sisters. Then, the voice said that she and her mother would be together with the king of hell, Yanlou, whereupon the woman died. In her widely read memoir, *The Woman Warrior*, Maxine Hong Kingston (b. 1940) refers to this form of infanticide, in which a box of clean ashes was prepared and kept beside the birth bed in case the child was a girl. Kingston quotes her mother, who was a midwife in China, as saying: "The midwife or relative would take the back of a girl baby's head in her hand and turn her face into the ashes. . . . It was very easy."[24]

The following stark description of infanticide appeared in a book published at Nanjing in 1874.

As soon as the little girls are born, they are plunged into the water in order to drown them or force is applied to their bodies in order to suffocate them or they are strangled with human hands. And something even more deplorable is that there are servants who place the girl in the chamber pot or in the basin used for the birth, which is still filled with water and blood and, shut away there, they die miserably. And what is even more monstrous is that if the mother is not cruel enough to take the life of her daughter, then her father-in-law, mother-in-law, or husband agitates her by their words to kill the girl.[25]

Palatre presented the Chinese texts and illustrations of one particularly striking story of a woman giving birth to a monster in three different versions (figs. 2.2, 2.3, and 2.4). However, he translated the text of only the popular morality version (fig. 2.2):

In the region situated to the north of the city of Danyang [on the Grand Canal in southern Jiangsu Province] lived a common man named Wang Sanyuan whose wife, surnamed Xu, had given birth to a son. The three children she later gave birth to were girls.

Irritated one day, he burst out with a curse and said to his wife: "You are good only to cause our ruin, in begetting only female merchandise (*cihuo*)." The wife Xu was obliged then to drown two of her daughters. Much later, at the time of a new birth, she was seized with an overwhelming pain, and remained three days [in labor] without delivering the child. Sanyuan called to heaven, and promised that thereafter none of the children born to them would be drowned. A voice suddenly spoke, coming out of the mother's womb and saying: "I have already been drowned by you two times; today I return to take life." Sanyuan asked for grace, but his prayer was useless; his wife then gave partial birth that day to a monster with a human head and the body of a snake. As the lower part of the body was unable to make its way out, she fainted into unconsciousness. Their son, aged seven years, also died of fright, and the angry old mother-in-law breathed her last breath. The father of the family rushed to the god of the hearth, prostrated his face against the earth, made a vow, and promised that in the future he would give himself to the Buddhist cause and exhort his fellow countrymen to save children. Then a spirit of radiant light, covered with armor of gold, appeared and, armed with a whip in his hand, removed the snake. The woman Xu, being dead, then returned to life by transmigration; she exhorted all those whom she encountered [about the evil of infanticide] and she consequently became the mother of a son. This event happened in the reign of Qianlong [1736–1796].[26]

This story of infanticide is infused with the morality of Buddhist karmic retribution. Although the description of the newborn child as a monster with a human head and body of a snake is bizarre, it is unlikely to have been pure fabrication because the didactic purpose of these stories would suffer if they seemed too far removed from people's everyday lives. More realistically, the infant the woman gave birth to in the story was probably

Figure 2.2. After having previously drowned two daughters (symbolized by the legs extending from the chamber pot), woman Xu is punished in karmic retribution by giving birth to a human-headed snake. This causes her, her prized son, as well as her mother-in-law (left) to all die of fright. The story is set in Danyang in Jiangsu Province. Liang-ki-koei, *Xuetang riji* (Suzhou, 1860) p. 38, reproduced in Palatre, *L'infanticide*, p. 58 & appendix #18.

malformed below the waist. The spirit of radiant light was probably Yan-luo, the king of hell. The tale was told as a moral aphorism and warning, as revealed in the illustration's Chinese caption, "The drowning of girls injures a son." The family (through the voices of the father and the mother-in-law) applied pressure on the mother to have a girl child killed and although the indications are that the mother would agree to the killing, we hear nothing from her.

溺女生怪

丹陽王氏連溺兩女一
婆罵一囙自己後生一怪。囙
蛇蟠腰裡老婆一嚇吐血
跌死小兒亦死大夫猶
淚道光去年八月之事

增壽一年

媳婦生
老婆常
寬報一如
送了老

小兒已死
了夾殺也
無用

佐證東
西希奇
古怪

阿呀阿呀
痛煞哉也

Figure 2.3. A nineteenth-century broadsheet variation on a woman giving birth to a monster in karmic retribution for drowning her daughters. Her mother-in-law and young son are shown coughing up blood and dying of fright while the father looks on helplessly. The story is set in Danyang in Jiangsu Province. Attached to Palatre, *L'infanticide*, p. 111. Widener Library, Harvard College Library, Ch 75.78F.

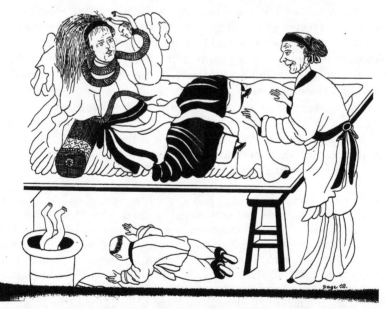

Figure 2.4. Another nineteenth-century broadsheet variation on the story of a woman giving birth to a monster in karmic retribution for drowning her daughters. Her mother-in-law is looking on in shock while her young son, dead from the shock, is lying on the floor. The legs extending from the chamber pot symbolize the daughters whom the mother previously drowned. The story is set in Jiangyin in Jiangsu province. Attached to Palatre, *L'infanticide*, p. 110. Widener Library, Harvard College Library, Ch 75.78F.

The mothers' voices are so absent from these tales that it is hard to know what their thoughts and feelings were, although their misgivings and sense of remorse are mentioned. Most of the writers were males and would have been, at best, only indirectly acquainted with the mother's feelings. Moreover, some of the illustrations of infanticide are misleading in that they depict the father, when in fact, normally only women were present in the birthing room and it would have been the mother who either drowned the newborn girl or told the midwife to do it.

We can glean some of the mothers' thoughts from written exhortations aimed at mothers. One such exhortation appeared in 1860 in a book filled with moral teachings that condemned certain acts, including infanticide, as immoral. It referred to "a type of unreasonable woman who having given birth to a daughter, then plunges her into a container of water and suffocates her."[27] The argument made against killing girls was based partly on the biological equality of boys and girls. However, the main thrust of the argument against killing girls in morality books lay in the retribution inflicted by Buddhist karma and involved a certain moral calculus. The drowning of one little girl would be punished by the death of a little boy. The drowning of two girls would be punished by the deaths of two boys. A husband who did not oppose the infanticide would have his life shortened by ten years. Neighbors and midwives who saw the drowning and did not oppose it would be punished in the same way.

Another feature commonly found in such popular tales is that the prayers to heaven were rarely answered in a positive way and seem to have been presented mainly as an expression of remorse. In the popular morality books, good deeds were rewarded and evil deeds were punished using a coldly rational logic in which forgiveness played no role. The karmic debt paid by mothers who drowned their girl children often involved a later difficult childbirth with prolonged labor pains. The following morality story makes this point.

> In Zhejiang Province, at Qingshan District, a woman had successively drowned five little girls. The sixth placed herself in a breeched position and refused to be born. The unfortunate mother suffered, as if she had been sliced in the body with a knife. Suddenly, a voice of an infant was heard in a wail: "I have already come five times into your body in order to take human form, and each time you have drowned me. Today, as before, I am still a girl; in being born, I believe I will have the same experience; so I would rather die in your body and make you die with me." These words were scarcely spoken when the poor woman uttered a cry and died.[28]

Buddhism was particularly vehement in punishing those who killed, and imposed karmic justice on those who practiced infanticide. The kings of the ten hells were regarded as personifications of King Yanluo (Yanluo wang), the supreme judge of the underworld who was derived from Yama,

Hindu god of the underworld.[29] In the Aryan hymns called the Vedas, Yama is the god of the dead with whom the spirits of the departed dwell. In Buddhism, he was said to preside over hell, either in the fifth court or by ruling the judges of all eighteen courts of hell. (The popular Buddhist-Daoist teaching of China conceived of hell in terms of either ten or eighteen divisions.) Buddhist hell differed from the Christian hell in the sense that the punishments lasted only one reincarnation rather than an eternity. The popular Chinese conception of King Yanluo as the judge of hell emphasized Buddhist elements, as the following story shows (fig. 2.5).

> At Dianbai District in the province of Guangdong, Zhang Da and his wife Ye burned incense without ceasing and addressed their prayers to the Buddha. After their death, the judge of purgatory, King Yanluo, condemned Zhang to be reincarnated as a pig and his wife as a dog. Zhang whined: "During our lives my wife and I loved and honored the Buddha; how can we be changed into beasts?" King Yanlou answered: "What use was there in continuing to offer homage to the Buddha? As to the three girls that you previously procreated, it was I who had sent them to earth, and nevertheless you had the

Figure 2.5.   The husband Zhang Da and his wife Ye practiced Buddhist devotions but sinned by drowning three daughters. For this they were punished in karmic retribution by the king of hell, who caused them to be reincarnated as a pig and dog so that they would be butchered as food. Ho-tong-tse, *Zhengying baoying lu* (reprinted 1869), p. 7, reproduced in Palatre, *L'infanticide*, p. 63 & appendix 24.

cruelty to drown them. Although you have the face of a man, you have the heart of a beast. I have to change you into an animal, so that on your return to earth, you will have your throat cut." When this sentence was pronounced, Zhang was transformed into the form of a pig and his wife into the form of a dog.[30]

Lactation (producing breast milk to suckle an infant) played a prominent role in infanticide. It was widely believed that breast-feeding delayed conception and if the woman was suckling a girl, this would delay the birth of the next child, who would hopefully be a boy. The following story captures this concern.

> At Jinhua District in Zhejiang Province, Chang Jinlan had a wife surnamed Yang who was thirty years of age. She gave birth first to a little girl, and he angrily said to her: "We will gain nothing by feeding this child; also, if you raise (i.e., breast-feed) her for three years, it will exhaust your *qi* (vital force) and delay another birth." And so he preferred to drown the girl in the hope of getting a boy. But during the night Chang Jinlan saw his father already dead in a dream. This old man with a voice choked with sobs said to him, "I have given birth to you and heaven intended for you to have a son. But because you have drowned your daughter, the king of hell has become very angry and has prevented the birth of this heir already promised by destiny; and now, deprived us of descendants." Chang Jinglan woke up, and related this dream to his wife, who had had the same dream. They remained childless down to the end of their lives; but their regrets were useless.[31]

An inability to lactate is sometimes presented as a punishment for infanticide, as in the following story (fig. 2.6).

> In the Suian District the woman Liu had given birth to two little girls and had drowned them one after another. She later gave birth to a boy and this birth filled her with joy. One day when she was feeding her child, she was suddenly knocked to the ground and saw in her confusion two little demons (*gui*) who seized her breasts and cruelly bit into them, while a great spirit cried to her, brandishing a knife: "The king of hell Yanluo remembers you snatching away life." Shortly thereafter she felt a dreadful pain in her bosom and her whole body putrefied. Over several days she uttered loud cries, then she expired. Her son, deprived of milk, was unable to survive her.[32]

Midwives (*wenpo*) acquired a tainted reputation through their role in drowning newborn children. The following moral tale (fig. 2.7) shows how they were regarded as fitting objects of karmic retribution.

> At Huanxishan [in Zhejiang Province?] a farmer woman surnamed Du taught the people how to drown their little girls and made a profit from rendering services of a similar nature. One day her husband went to the mountain to gather fuel and was devoured by a tiger. In the evening when he failed to return home, a neighbor said that they had seen traces of blood on the path of the mountain. His wife was eager for his return. She followed these traces

Figure 2.6. Woman Liu, who previously had drowned her two daughters, was pun-ished in karmic retribution by the king of hell by having two demonic reincarnations of her daughters bite her breasts, causing her body to putrefy. When she died, her son (ly-ing at her feet) died from a lack of breast milk. *Guobao tu*, one of four volumes that compose *Zhuyu yuan* (Shanghai, undated), p. 8, reproduced in Palatre, *L'infanticide*, p. 74 & appendix 33.

of blood and saw her husband in the mouth of a tiger. She herself was at-tacked by the claws of this animal and she received a wound which immedi-ately paralyzed her. The proverb says: "The tiger does not devour its young; and the man who is not like him, deserves to fall into his teeth."[33]

教溺虎噬

Figure 2.7. Farm woman Du was punished in karmic retribution for teaching rural people how to drown their little girls and for making a profit over their deaths. A tiger killed her husband and attacked her. Ho-tong-tse, *Zhengying baoying lu* (reprinted 1869), p. 5, reproduced in Palatre, *L'infanticide*, p. 73 & appendix 32.

Sometimes the stories tell of gruesome but fitting punishments being inflicted on midwives, as in the following story (fig. 2.8).

At Longnan District in Jiangxi Province there lived a midwife surnamed Liu who made a practice of drowning little girls. One night she saw in a dream the king of hell, Yanluo, who ordered his assistants to cut out her tongue, and he made this reproach: "You have the practice of helping parents drown their little girls. These children who are plunged into the water are unable to complain. Alas! Why have you not been willing to spare them?" At these words, woman Liu awoke. Her tongue was swollen. It putrefied and caused her great pain. She suffered from hunger for one month and died. In dying, she was heard to make a cry like a goat.[34]

Figure 2.8. The bad midwife Liu was punished in karmic retribution for drowning little girls. The king of hell has her tongue cut out, creating an infection that caused her to die. Ho-tong-tse, *Zhengying baoying lu* (reprinted 1869), p. 8, reproduced in Palatre, *L'infanticide*, p. 65 & appendix 25.

However, there were also cases of good midwives who opposed infanticide, such as midwife Li (fig. 2.9):

> At Hejian Prefecture in Zhili Province [south of Beijing] there lived, close to a venerable age, the happy matron Li. She was a skilled midwife and in spite of the heat and cold, she never refused to go, when someone came to ask for help. She encouraged the women in the midst of their suffering, . . . and, when a mother wanted to drown her little girl, she used all her eloquence to prevent her from committing this crime. She sought out a wet nurse to whom she gave the child by which she saved its life. Thanks to these acts of charity, she enjoyed a happy old age, and died at the age of eighty-three years. She herself saw her son and her five grandsons enjoy a great reputation, and today some of them are still scholar-officials.[35]

As with midwives, neighbor women could play either a good or bad role in dealing with infanticide. Woman Li is presented as a bad example (fig. 2.10):

> At Fuan District in Fujian Province there lived a common man named Chen Liangyi. His wife surnamed Lin, who was very close with her neighbor woman Li, brought two girls into the world. Mrs. Li carried the water in order to help Mrs. Lin drown the girls and so also took part in this crime. However, she soon contracted an illness; and in her deliriousness she saw in her dream her father-in-law and mother-in-law, who said to her in crying: "We have chosen you to be the wife of our son, in order to perpetuate the line of our ancestors, and heaven destined you to have two boys. Why have you helped Mrs. Lin to drown her daughters in carrying the water for her? You have stopped by your own hand the continuation of our descendants." In punishment for this crime, she had no more children.[36]

As with the midwives, a story of a bad neighbor woman was contrasted with a story of a good neighbor woman in order to teach a moral lesson (fig. 2.11):

> In Taiping District in the Jiangnan region (Anhui Province), there lived a man named Jin Zuo. His wife Ying brought a little girl into the world and wanted to drown her. The neighbor woman Zhuang persuaded her absolutely not to be culpable of such a crime, and during the night she had a dream of a spirit who told her: "Today in opposing an infanticide, and in saving the life of a little girl, you were truly in accord with heaven and earth, who live to give life. The Lord Above (*Shangdi*) is happy with your conduct, and will give you one day a son who will become famous." At these words Mrs. Zhuang awoke, and recounted this vision to her husband. That same year she gave birth to a son, who, while still young, was recognized as a scholar and by a series of fortunate successes in his exams, acquired the rank of *shengyuan* (licentiate or lowest degree).[37]

餘慶堂

李穩婆

Figure 2.9.   The good midwife Li was rewarded in karmic recompense for preventing the drowning of newborn girls and given a long life with five grandsons who became successful scholar-officials. *Cihang pudu ce* (reprinted in Tongzhi reign [1862-1874]), reproduced in Palatre, *L'infanticide*, p. 27 & appendix 37.

Figure 2.10. Mrs. Li (left) helped her neighbor Mrs. Lin drown two newborn girls and was punished in karmic retribution by being denied the sons she had been destined to have. Ho-tong-tse, *Zhengying baoying lu* (reprinted 1869), p. 12, reproduced in Palatre, *L'infanticide*, p. 68 & appendix 27.

A similar story with a slight variation was set in the Putian District in Fujian Province (figs. 2.12 and 2.13). After giving birth to a girl, the mother ordered her sister-in-law to bring water for drowning. The neighbor woman Lin urged them not to drown the girl and took the child in her arms. The struggling infant's legs sticking out of the chamber pot in figure 2.12 indicate that Mrs. Lin intervened to lift the child out of the chamber pot where it was being drowned. A spirit (depicted above Mrs. Lin's head) observed this. The male spirit figure is dressed in purple clothing and carrying a book. The color purple was associated with both heaven and the emperor, and this appears to represent the Daoist god of literature, Wenchang Dijun.

This god is said to have originated as a man named Zhang Yazi, who lived at Qiqu Mountain in Sichuan. He was an official in the Jin dynasty (265–420) and died on the battlefield.[38] He was reincarnated repeatedly in

阻
溺
獲
福
圖

Figure 2.11.   Mrs. Zhuang (right) persuaded her neighbor Mrs. Ying not to drown her newborn girl and was rewarded through karmic recompense with a son who attained a scholarly degree. Ho-tong-tse, *Zhengying baoying lu* **(reprinted 1869), p. 14, reproduced in Palatre,** *L'infanticide,* **p. 69 & appendix 28.**

the Tang and Song dynasties and a temple was built for him and sacrifices offered. He was deified in the Yuan dynasty in 1314. As a spirit, he was initially known as Zitong Dijun, but later acquired the name of Wenchang Dijun (god of literature). He is usually depicted holding a writing brush and book with four characters meaning "Heaven determines literary success." The common people believed that the god of literature had the power to reward examinees with success on the literary exams. Although a Daoist deity, he was eclectic in promoting all Three Teachings (Buddhism, Confucianism, and Daoism).[39] The spirit secured the future success of Mrs. Lin's son, who passed the exams and became a great scholar-official.[40] In the iconography of these popular illustrations, the god of literature has a parallel function to the king of hell. Each has a meaning attached to his pictorial representation. Whereas the appearance of Yan-luo represents karmic punishment for the evil act of killing a girl, the appearance of Wenchang Dijun represents the karmic reward of examination success for the good deed of saving a girl.

阻
溺
感
神

Figure 2.12.   When a mother ordered her sister-in-law to drown her newborn girl, the neighbor woman Lin (right) intervened to save the child. The god of literature (depicted above her head) observed this and secured the future success of Mrs. Lin's son as a scholar-official. *Guobao tu*, one of four volumes that compose *Zhuyu yuan*, (Shanghai, undated), p. 2, reproduced in Palatre, *L'infanticide*, p. 76 & appendix 35.

救溺神記

惜字一千

安陳氏鄰同溺女。
婦王氏力勸阻止。
說不可助他錢米。
明晰記忽生貴子。
試文章主考丟棄。
聞不可乃再拾起。
了舉人聯捷進。
康熙年間浙江
事救人一命。報
如此。

Figure 2.13. A broadsheet variation on the theme of a good neighbor woman intervening with food and money to prevent the drowning of a newborn girl. The god of literature (above her head) observed this and rewarded her son with success in the scholar-official examinations. Attached to Palatre, *L'infanticide*, p. 111. Widener Library, Harvard College Library, Ch 75.78F.

CONFUCIANISM IN POPULAR MORALITY LITERATURE

For fourteen hundred years, until 1905, the traditional path to success in Chinese society was through the civil service examinations. Following intensive study of the Confucian Classics, the candidate undertook a series of examinations at the local, provincial, and national levels. Success at even the lowest level bestowed local elite status on the degree holder while success at the higher levels brought appointment as a scholar-official and with it, the rewards of power, prestige, and wealth. Successful candidates tended to invest their wealth in family landholdings, and during periods of dismissal or retirement from active service, they returned to the family landholdings to become part of the local gentry elite. This local gentry elite was called on to provide moral leadership and financial support in the fight against infanticide.

The popular moral literature (*shanshu*) presented cases of literati who actively opposed infanticide and were rewarded with success on the examinations. These stories were not aimed at an upper-class audience. Their emphasis on the practical rewards of status and wealth that examination success offered indicates that the main audience of these moralistic stories was the poor and humble people who dreamed of becoming literati. The didactic purposes of this popular literature required a pairing of good and bad examples in each category involving infanticide, and so examples of good and bad literati were added to those of mothers, fathers, midwives, and neighbors. The literatus Peng Zhuangyuan of the Zhangzhou District of Suzhou in Jiangsu Province was said to be active in feeding infants of poor families.[41] He prevented infanticides by informing himself about poor families who were on the verge of committing infanticide. Each month, he contributed money and rice to these families that enabled them to feed their newborn children. He also wrote a literary composition against infanticide. Peng was rewarded for his work in saving girls from infanticide by the examination success of his sons and grandsons, who became members of the prestigious Hanlin Academy in Beijing. He and his descendants enjoyed long and prosperous lives (fig. 2.14).

Peng's negative counterpart was Huang Guilin of Xiushui District in Zhejiang Province (fig. 2.15).[42] While Peng promoted good deeds, Huang mocked good deeds. He impeded those who sought to establish orphanages and protective societies. At his examinations, he hallucinated and innumerable small hands appeared to distract his attention. He threatened these creatures with a knife and died, swallowing his tongue. The innumerable small hands in this account appear to represent the spirits of the little girls who died because of his opposition and returned to haunt him. One might also interpret the incident to represent the effects of Huang's guilty conscience, or a stress-induced seizure in which his tongue was swallowed.

Efforts to save girls from infanticide were presented as an exemplary form of behavior that could raise the status of an otherwise obscure literatus to prominence. This was the case with Li Zongyi of Xinchang District (probably in western Jiangxi Province).[43] Li was a licentiate (*xiucai*), or lowest degree holder who failed to earn advanced degrees; however, the local history of his hometown, Xinchang, lists him as being first in moral behavior. It began when he found an abandoned infant girl floating in a stream under a bridge. He retrieved her with a boat hook (gaff) and gave her to his wife to raise as a future daughter-in-law. When his wife's breast milk was exhausted, Li paid a wet nurse five hundred copper cash each month to nurse the girl. Copper cash (*qian*) were square copper coins with a hole in the middle that allowed them to be strung together. In the Qing dynasty, approximately one thousand copper cash represented one tael (*liang*) of unminted silver, which weighed 1.1 ounces (31.25 grams).

When Li's generosity became known, others brought little girls to him to care for and he is said to have treated them like his own daughters. Other people came seeking wives from among these girls. Li subsidized other poor families so that they could raise their own daughters. When he was overwhelmed by their needs, he solicited contributions from relatives and friends and in this way he was credited with saving three hundred or four hundred little girls.

救嬰榮顯

Figure 2.14. The literatus Peng Zhuangyuan was rewarded through karmic recompense for his work in combating female infanticide with a long, prosperous life and the success of his sons and grandsons as scholar-officials. *Guobao tu*, one of four volumes that compose *Zhuyu yuan* (Shanghai, undated), reproduced in Palatre, *L'infanticide*, p. 70 & appendix 29.

阻善斃命

Figure 2.15.   The examination candidate Huang Guilin was punished through karmic retribution for mocking and obstructing efforts to save girls from infanticide. He was subjected to hallucinations involving demonic reincarnations of murdered girls which disrupted his examination and led to his death. *Guobao tu*, one of four volumes that compose *Zhuyu yuan* (Shanghai, undated), p. 5, reproduced in Palatre, *L'infanticide*, p. 72 & appendix 31.

The popular morality tales of literati sometimes mixed realism and fantasy. Father Gabriel Palatre recounted two of these stories involving the god of literature, who presided over the literary essays in the examinations. The lighter of these two stories featured Wang Xuan of Mianyang in Hubei Province.[44] Wang exhorted his fellow countrypeople not to drown newborn girls. Sometimes he gave money and rice to dissuade peasants from killing their daughters. When a family refused to agree to save the girl, he took the child to his home and found a midwife to nurse her. He sold several plots of his land to fund these activities. In 1794, he went to take the examinations and found lodgings in a Buddhist monastery where he was welcomed by a monk. That night, Wang had a dream in which he met the god of literature. The spirit congratulated Wang on his activities to save newborn girls from death, but expressed dissatisfaction with the features of his face. In order to improve Wang's appearance, the spirit bestowed a full beard on him. When the welcoming monk saw Wang's beard the next morning, he was amazed (fig. 2.16). When the list of successful exam candidates was posted, Wang's name was ranked first.

A more serious story involving the god of literature featured the aspiring literatus Gui Zhongfu of Wuling (near Hangzhou) and his friend Chen Xiting.[45] In this story, the god of literature clearly promoted those literati who combatted female infanticide. Gui had written an essay opposing female infanticide, but he had not followed through on his intention to publish it. When Gui's friend Chen divined to inquire about Gui's chances of success in the exams, the god of literature answered that he had removed Gui's name from the list of successful candidates because of Gui's failure to distribute his essay. Chen begged to intervene on his friend's behalf and did so, with the result that the essay was published.

Palatre reprinted only the preface to Gui's essay. Prefaces were normally written by colleagues and friends, and in this case, Chen was the author. Palatre presented a summary rather than a translation of Gui's arguments against infanticide, perhaps because the strangeness and difficulty of the material frustrated the Jesuit's ability to translate it word for word. Neo-Confucianism placed great emphasis on the harmonious interaction of all the elements of nature. Human procreation constituted an important part of this interaction, and female infanticide represented disharmony with nature. Chen cited tigers, wolves, ants, phoenixes, and unicorns as species who preserved their young, and he contrasted this preservation with humans who killed newborn girls. Furthermore, humans were fickle in their sympathies. They pitied a little chick that died from a crushed eggshell or a piglet that died in birth, but they had no sympathy for the little girls whom they drowned. The preface warned families about the dangers of self-destruction and cited the proverb, "A

Figure 2.16. The examination candidate Wang Xuan was rewarded in 1794 for his work in combating female infanticide by having the god of literature (not pictured) improve his appearance with a full beard. The change was noticed by the Buddhist monk guest-keeper. Liang-ki-koei, *Xuetang riji* **(Suzhou, 1860), p. 29, reproduced in Palatre,** *L'in-fanticide,* **p. 56 & appendix 17.**

family that fails to nurture girls for three generations will be extermi-nated." Literati were exhorted to serve as models by establishing foundling hospices and feeding newborn girls who had been abandoned.

The popular didactic literature influenced by Buddhist and Daoist morality combated infanticide with rewards (health, long life, birth of sons, examination success, and wealth) and punishments (illness, suffer-ing, failure, and death) that might appear in this world or in the next world through reincarnation. By contrast, the literati adopted a more pa-ternalistic approach of dealing with the poor and uneducated people through legal prohibitions and financial assistance.[46] Their approach in-volved rewards and punishments that were more Legalist than Confucian in character.

Literati who emphasized this approach often failed to recognize that affluent families were also guilty of infanticide. One of the documents on the regulations of an infant protection society discussed how the concubines conspired with the wives of affluent families to kill newborn girls. It is one of the few documents that refer to the mother's feelings, as follows:

> The prohibition against drowning little girls is addressed above all to the poor, but no attention at all is paid to the rich and noble, who when they reach middle age without male children are rendered guilty of this crime. The wife believes then that one may introduce concubines into the family. They want to do everything possible to bring a boy into the world in order to win the good graces of the husband. And so the legitimate wife and the concubine conceive of the desire to drown the little girls. Moreover, the father-in-law and mother-in-law wish to have little boys with brief delays. The husband dreams only of having descendants, and when a girl comes into the world, everyone feels pity and expresses only sadness. The mother, devastated by chagrin, becomes ill; her sorrow is changed into cruelty, and the desire is born to drown the little girls.[47]

POPULAR BROADSHEETS AND NEWSPAPERS

The anti-infanticide literature of nineteenth-century China comprised four different literary forms, each geared to the different levels of literacy among the Chinese people. The literati essays condemning infanticide used a sophisticated vocabulary and literary allusions that only highly educated Chinese could comprehend. The second form, the popular morality literature, also required a fairly extensive vocabulary of its readers. However, most people in China at that time were either illiterate or semiliterate. If we define literacy as the ability to read and write a few hundred characters, then probably only 30–45 percent of men and 2–10 percent of women were literate in the last half of the nineteenth century.[48] For many people, broadsheets with illustrations were the most effective medium, both in terms of communicating a simpler message and in being less expensive. This represented a third literary form. In comparison with the illustrations in the popular morality works, the broadsheet illustrations were more detailed and the accompanying descriptions were simpler. Newspapers were the fourth literary form.

Six nineteenth-century broadsheets opposing infanticide were reproduced and bound as folded leaves in *L'infanticide* because Palatre believed they were further evidence of the widespread nature of infanticide.[49] These broadsheet illustrations reflect a more sophisticated artistic style than the illustrations reproduced in the text of *L'infanticide*. Perhaps this was because the orphan printers at the mission press of Zikawei had re-copied original drawings, causing a loss of aesthetic quality. Each broad-sheet contains one to four illustrations portraying the consequences of how one responded to infanticide. Those who intervene to save girl ba-bies are rewarded. Local gentry and merchants receive honors and long lives. Midwives and neighbors are rewarded with the birth of sons, many descendants, and wealth. Brothers receive examination success and high status. By contrast, those who drown baby girls give birth to freaks, see their sons die, and sometimes lose their own lives.

Broadsheets were published with as many as four, six, eight, or ten dif-ferent scenes and appealed to the curiosity of the buyer. These connected illustrations (*lianhuan tuhua*) were forerunners of modern Chinese car-toons.[50] They originated in the Six Dynasties period (222–589) with a sin-gle illustration for a story, but over the years increased the number of il-lustrations used in depicting a story. Like illustrated magazines and tabloid newspapers today, they appealed to people as light reading. Sev-eral of these illustrated stories presented simplified versions of infanticide stories found in the popular morality books. The stories they portrayed were probably circulating in oral traditions that were adapted by both the popular morality books and broadsheets. While some broadsheets appear to have been moneymaking projects, others were distributed at cost as part of a benevolent effort to save baby girls from infanticide. The pub-lishers of a new edition of *A Display of Punishments Inflicted on Those Who Drown Little Girls* (1874) regarded propagation of their book as a work of religious merit. To facilitate propagation, they offered to print and sell their book for nothing but the cost of the paper.[51]

These broadsheets presented two additional versions of the sensational story involving the birth of a human-headed snake (figs. 2.3 and 2.4). The basic features of these two versions are the same as the story in the popu-lar morality book; however, the details vary. The morality tale version (fig. 2.2) and one broadsheet version (fig. 2.3) are both set in the city of Danyang on the Grand Canal in southern Jiangsu Province while the other broadsheet version (fig. 2.4) is set in the Jiangyin District approxi-mately fifty miles to the east (see map 2). The morality tale version and the Danyang broadsheet version involve the Wang family (Wang Sanyuan and wife Xu), while the Jiangyin broadsheet version involves the Li fam-ily (Li Huichu). The morality tale version dates these events to the Qian-long reign (1736–1796); the Danyang broadsheet version dates them to 1827; and the Jiangyin broadsheet version is undated.

The morality tale and Danyang broadsheet versions claim that two daughters have been drowned while the Jiangyin broadsheet version claims that three daughters have been drowned. All three versions por-tray the scolding mother-in-law, although only the morality tale and

Danyang broadsheet versions describe her in their texts. Only the Jiangying version describes this monstrosity suckling at the woman's breast for three days, while the Danyang broadsheet version is the only version to illustrate this suckling. Only the Jiangyin version text contains the dying wife's insistence that the husband participate in an infant protection society (*baoying hui*) and contribute money for the support of poor infants.

There is also a difference in intellectual tenor among the three versions. The Jiangyin version is the most sophisticated in terms of presenting Buddhist teachings that underlie karmic retribution. It is also the only version of this story to claim that the charitable act of contributing to an infant protection society can redeem the parents from the sin of having drowned their daughters. The dying Mrs. Li tells her husband that only this will release her from being reincarnated in the lake of blood (*xue chi*). This lake of blood was part of the eighteenth hell—the hell of cold ice—the last of the eighteen hells of popular Chinese Buddhism.[52] This hell was for women who had given birth, and is linked with the widespread ancient belief that the blood of menstruation and childbirth was a dangerous pollutant.

The morality tale is the only one of the three versions of the human-headed snake story to refer to the king of hell, Yanluo. The Danyang broadsheet version appealed to the broadest audience by simplifying the text and enhancing the dramatic aspects of the illustration, including the vomiting mother-in-law and little son, the spilled chamber pot, and the weeping father. These different versions might reflect similar births of malformed infants that occurred at different times and in different places or they might reflect how an event was changed in certain details by being circulated in oral form (much as a striking piece of gossip is transmitted by word of mouth) before being recorded in written form. The slightly different mix of fantasy and realism in these three versions shows that they were imaginative enough to attract attention but realistic enough to be believable. They represent a form of folk literature aimed at discouraging the killing of newborn girls.

A second theme from the popular morality books that is repeated in the broadsheets is the good midwife who saves the life of a baby girl by persuading the mother not to drown the child. However, once again, the details of the broadsheet illustrations differ from the morality book stories. One story is set in the town of Liyang in Jiangsu Province and involves a midwife named Mrs. Fan (fig. 2.17). She makes a vow before a spirit to save baby girls and she offers poor mothers money and food if they spared their child. The illustration displays a chamber pot with a lid removed placed prominently in the foreground to indicate that the infant would have been drowned had she not been spared through the persuasive force of midwife Fan. The mother is shown carrying the infant toward

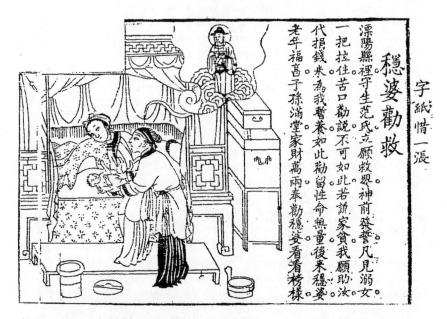

Figure 2.17. A broadsheet variation on the theme of a good midwife who was rewarded through karmic recompense. Mrs. Fan fulfilled her vow to the god of literature (shown above her head) by intervening with money and rice to prevent the drowning of a baby girl. Attached to Palatre, *L'infanticide*, p. 111. Widener Library, Harvard College Library, Ch 75.78F.

the chamber pot while Mrs. Fan restrains her. The god of literature appears above Mrs. Fan's head to observe that she has fulfilled her vow to save baby girls. In her old age, midwife Fan is rewarded with family wealth and enough descendants to fill the ancestral temple.

A third theme from the popular morality books (figs. 2.11 and 2.12) repeated in a broadsheet (fig. 2.13) is the good neighbor woman who intervenes to save a newborn girl from death.[53] Like the midwife, the neighbor woman uses persuasion and the offer of money and food to help save the child. The god of literature observes her good deed and rewards the neighbor woman with examination success for a son. The story portrayed in this broadsheet illustration duplicates one of the morality book tales (fig. 2.12) with a story from the examination setting. When this son takes his exam for the second (*zhuren*) degree, the examiner is on the verge of rejecting the son's essay when he hears a voice saying, "You cannot," which is exactly what the son's mother said years before to the woman about to drown her newborn daughter. Because of this voice, the examiner passes the essay and the son goes on to attain the highest (*jinshi*) degree. The broadsheet account is said to have happened in Zhejiang Province during the Kangxi reign (1662–1722) while the corresponding popular morality tale is undated and set in the Putian District of Fujian Province.

Chinese filial piety insisted on such a degree of obedience from a child that disobedience was punishable as a criminal act. Opposing a parent's wishes to drown a baby sister presented a challenge to this moral code. Nevertheless, one of the broadsheets presents a case of such intervention as a meritorious act that was rewarded with academic degrees (fig. 2.18). There was a son named Yu Rixin of Shaoxing in Zhejiang Province.[54] When he heard that his mother wanted to drown his newborn sister, he fell to his knees and, weeping, begged his mother not to drown her. Perhaps the dead daughter would return and ask for his life in return. The parents listened to their son and spared their daughter's life. The god of literature is depicted hovering over the son's head, symbolizing the son's eventual reward in attaining third place in the list of successful candidates at the palace examination. In addition, Yu Rixin attained unparalleled wealth, honors, and longevity.

Several of the broadsheet stories were not discussed by Palatre, but the common repetition of the accounts makes it likely that they too were reproduced elsewhere in the voluminous popular morality literature. Two of them deal with benevolent local gentry who gave money and food to poor women so that they would not be forced to drown their daughters. In the first, Zhang Gongrui not only enjoyed a long life of eighty years because of his contributions, but he also received the honor of a visit from a Hanlin scholar whose mother had been saved by Zhang's efforts. The second story involved an unnamed gentleman of Nanchang in Jiangxi Province. When the gentleman was forty-seven years old, a physiognomist predicted on the basis of his body shape that he would have a short life. But then, through his monetary aid to women in childbirth during a famine, the gentleman saved the lives of many children and was rewarded with a long life.

Sometimes the amount of detail in the stories gives them a greater historical basis. One of these apparently more historical broadsheet stories about the consequences of female infanticide tells of Chen Da, who lived in the market town of Shatou (in the administrative area of Taicang), a region only thirty miles northwest of Shanghai.[55] Life was good for Chen Da. He had opened a small shop that was thriving and he had four sons. However, his wife had also given birth to four girls, each of whom the couple had drowned. Chen bragged that he had disposed of the nuisance of raising girls. When the eldest son was thirty-three, the other sons were twenty-seven, twenty-four, and thirteen. They were all married and regarded as fortunate men. However, in 1838 they all contracted smallpox. Both Chen

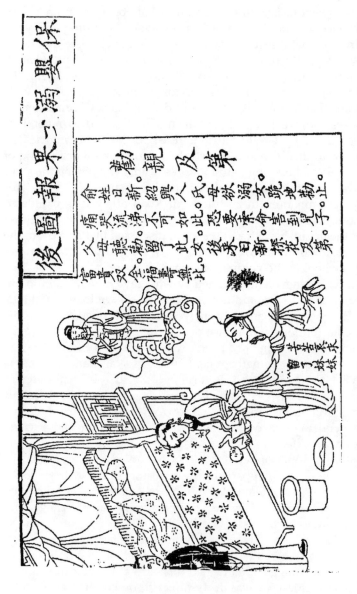

Figure 2.18. A broadsheet depiction of how a son's tears and pleading saved his younger sister from being drowned. The god of literature (above his head) noted his good deed and secured his success in the scholar-official examinations. Attached to Palatre, *L'infanticide*, p. 111. Widener Library, Harvard College Library, Ch 75.78F.

Figure 2.19. A broadsheet illustration of the shopkeeper Chen Da and his wife of Sha-tou in the Taicang area. He raised four sons but drowned his four daughters (portrayed as demonic ghosts). In spite of his prosperity and good fortune, heaven inflicted retribution on him when all four of his sons (only three are portrayed) contracted smallpox and died in 1838. Attached to Palatre, *L'infanticide*, p. 109. Widener Library, Harvard College Library, Ch 75.78F.

Da and his wife dreamed that four demons (*gui*) appeared, demanding the sons' lives (fig. 2.19). The demons represented the drowned daughters. Over a period of two months, all four sons died from the smallpox. Soon afterward the mother died of grief. Chen grew old alone and without progeny. When he died in 1860, there was no one to bury him, and his rotting corpse was eaten by dogs. The broadsheet ends by admonishing readers that Chen Da's selfishness in killing his daughters cost the lives of his entire family. It urges people to repent and change their behavior before it is too late—because nothing escapes the eyes of heaven.

The new journalistic medium of newspapers was a fourth literary form believed by Palatre to confirm the widespread existence of infanticide. The international city of Shanghai provided a fertile setting for the development of early Chinese newspapers. (Although the *Beijing Gazette* [*Jing-bao*] had existed for centuries, it was more of a government-controlled record of official acts than a newspaper in the modern sense.) The *Shenbao* was the most important of these early newspapers, publishing from 1872 until 1905.[56] It was founded as a purely commercial venture by the investments of four British businessmen and was managed by a young man who was in his early thirties at the time of the founding. This man, Ernest Major (Mei Cha; 1841–1908), had quickly acquired fluency in spoken and written Chinese. Although the *Shenbao* was foreign owned, its readership consisted of literate Chinese.[57] Chinese both wrote it and read it, and it was a hybrid of a foreign journalistic form adapted to Chinese tastes. Because of the great autonomy enjoyed by the International Settlement in Shanghai, the *Shenbao* was remarkably free of interference by either the British consulate or the Qing court. This daily newspaper acquired a national readership.

Occasionally Palatre included an incidence of infanticide that seems to belong to a category of killing completely different from other forms of infanticide. He reproduced an article from the *Shenbao* describing a horrific case of infanticide that took place on May 9, 1878, on the riverfront in Ningbo.[58] A Chinese traveler reported that he had come across a crowd of several hundred curious people who were watching the burning of an infant girl. He heard the wails coming out of the smoke and watched as the child's charred body and bone were attached to a stone and sunk in the river. The child had been the third daughter of a blacksmith, and the other two daughters had also been killed. The child was burned in order to inspire terror in her soul and vital spirits that would prevent it from returning in another reincarnation. Unfortunately, this incident does nothing to prove Palatre's argument that infanticide was commonplace and ordinary in China. On the contrary, by presenting an incident that was included in a Chinese newspaper because of its sensational nature, Palatre contradicted his own argument.

3

✛

Official and Literati Efforts to Combat Infanticide

EARLY OFFICIAL EFFORTS TO COMBAT INFANTICIDE

It should be clear by this point that the role of Confucianism in regard to infanticide was by no means clear-cut. On one hand, Confucianism encouraged female infanticide by honoring age over youth and males over females. And yet the cruelty of drowning girls is at odds with the fundamental Confucian value of Benevolence (*Ren*) enunciated by Confucius (ca. 551–479 BC) himself. One might compare Confucianism's attitude toward infanticide to the conflicted role of Christianity in regard to slavery. Although some Christians claimed that African slavery was justified by certain passages from the Bible, others argued that it was a violation of the fundamental teaching of love that Jesus preached.

The earliest organized efforts to combat infanticide in China appear to date from the Song dynasty. The measures that Su Dongbo suggested in 1080 to the Huangzhou magistrate for dealing with the problem anticipated later efforts by local elites during the Qing dynasty. Su claimed that the law prescribed a punishment of two years' hard labor for anyone who willfully killed his descendant. He urged the magistrate to be more stringent in enforcing this law by posting it in official notices on walls and offering rewards to those who reported such crimes. The money for the reward was to come from fining the parent who committed the crime and from the neighbors in the *baojia* (collective responsibility) unit. If the parent was a tenant farmer, his landlord was also to be held culpable.

In addition to punishing those who broke the law, Su recommended to the magistrate that an active program of assistance from the richer families of the area to the poorer families would reduce the incidence of infanticide. Su himself organized an infant protection society and persuaded his neighbor, a philanthropic scholar named Gu Gengdao, to serve as its president. The association collected dues from wealthy people, asking them to contribute at least ten taels of silver per year plus rice, cloth, and cotton for quilts. Society representatives visited expectant mothers in the countryside and gave them presents of money, food, and clothing if they promised not to kill their infants.

A Southern Song government edict of 1133 condemned to two years in prison those who abandoned their children.[1] Those who killed their children were condemned to three years of imprisonment. As was often the case with proscriptions against infanticide, these laws either had little effect or were not implemented because they failed to deal with a fundamental cause of infanticide, which was poverty. In 1138, the government addressed this root cause of infanticide by offering money and food to poor families giving birth to children. Shortly afterward, in Fujian Province, the great Neo-Confucian philosopher Zhu Xi (1130–1200), who had developed the idea of communal granaries (*shecang*), conceived of "granaries for bearing children" (*juzicang*). The purpose of these granaries was to distribute food to parents too poor to feed their children.

The Bureau of Childhood Mercy (*Ciyouju*) was founded in 1247–1248 in Hangzhou by two literati and spread to Suzhou, Fuzhou, and elsewhere. These bureaus were supposed to gather poor children who had been orphaned or abandoned and to recruit wet nurses, who were lodged and fed at the bureau, to feed them. The government was to make monthly contributions of money, rice, and cloth in order to feed and clothe the children. The bureau was supposed to place the children up for adoption by families and to subsidize each adopted child with a stipend of a string of copper cash and three *dou* (one *dou* = ten liters) of rice each month until the child turned three years old. Unfortunately, these bureaus did not function effectively, mainly because the people preferred to either commit infanticide or place unwanted children in a monastery.

In spite of Marco Polo's claims, there is little corroborating evidence that foundling hospices for children existed during the Yuan dynasty (1279–1368). Although Mongol rulers prescribed harsh punishments for infanticide, it is not clear if such punishments were ever applied.[2] The government of the Ming dynasty (1368–1644) did not establish orphanages, but rather focused its efforts on assisting the elderly. There are numerous references in popular Ming literature to monasteries harboring children, including taking in the Ming founder Zhu Yuanzhang. Even more famous is the fictionalized story of the historical Buddhist monk Xuancang (Hsüan-tsang) in the folk novel *Journey to the West* (*Xi yu ji*) by Wu Chengen (ca. 1500–1582). According to the novel, Xuancang's mother, forced to abandon him, placed him in the river on a floating plank. He was found by an abbot who dubbed him "River Float" and raised him in the monastery.[3] However, the facts were more prosaic. The most common procedure in the Ming era for getting rid of unwanted children was infanticide.

EARLY QING LITERATI EFFORTS
TO ASSIST ABANDONED CHILDREN

The Qing dynasty (1644–1911) saw a new development in the treatment of abandoned children.[4] Beginning in 1655–1656, local elites (degree-holding gentry and merchants) took the initiative in establishing foundling hospices (*yuying tang*). Whereas Song orphanages had been run by the central government, Qing orphanages were private institutions run by local elites. The Qing court was not very decisive in dealing with infanticide, and orphanages had been established at Yangzhou in 1655–1656 prior to the first Qing edict condemning infanticide in 1659. The Kangxi emperor issued an edict on infanticide in 1673, thirteen years after the establishment of an orphanage at Beijing. The first Manchu emperor to really encourage orphanages was Yongzheng, who issued a decree in 1724.[5] His decree seems to have been the impetus for the establishment of eleven new orphanages in the Lower Yangzi River region in 1724–1734. Yet even his active support did not change the fact that local elites were far more active in aiding abandoned children than were the central and provincial governments.

One of the leading literary voices of the eighteenth century spoke out against female infanticide in a poem. Jiang Shiquan (1725–1785) of Nanchang in Jiangxi Province was the greatest playwright of his age and also one of its greatest poets.[6] His mother provided his early education and he remained unusually devoted to her throughout his lifetime. Although he attained the highest academic degree (*jinshi*) in 1757, he never achieved great success as an official and retired early, citing poor health. In his later years, he had extensive contact with the famous poet Yuan Mei and wrote his greatest literary works late in life.

Jiang's poem condemning female infanticide is part of a set of three poems praising the official Ouyang Lanqi for his petition. Ouyang petitioned the throne in 1736 to prohibit three practices then current in Jiangxi Province: the stopping of funerals, drowning girls, and imprisoning female servants.[7] Ironically, Jiang based his argument on the very same *Book of Odes* (*Shijing*) ode (Mao number 189) often cited to show Chinese inequity in the treatment of boys and girls (see chapter 1). While the ode can be interpreted as treating boys and girls differently, Jiang interprets it as nevertheless valuing both boys and girls. If the birth of a girl is also auspicious, drowning her is wrong. Jiang's poem follows.[8]

> Fortunate dream: omen of the snakes!
> Scepter? Wheel? Equally prized in the *Poems*![9]
> So why, a girl-child being auspicious,
> Should dad and mom think her an enemy?
> "Wa, Wa. . . !" She's pulled from mom's body
> And then—just like a stone thrown in a pond!
> They kill her in less than a moment,
> And there she dies—right in the chamber pot!
> Dad?—Flesh-ripping demon Aṅgulimālya!
> Mom?—The ghoul, Mātaṅga![10]
> Birds, vermin
>   take hard the early death of their issue;
> How much the more, creatures that grow hair?
> Humans glutted with venomous heartlessness,
> How can this murderous evil be stopped at all?
> But, ah! His Excellency, Master Ouyang,
> So tenderly pities the newborn babe!
> His proclamation sternly prohibits the practice,
> And his measures are spreading to neighboring districts.
> Give birth to a boy, you call him a "Shao" or "Du";[11]
> Give birth to a girl, and this is how you treat her?
> —If this decadent custom is going to be transformed,
> Let all of us now call upon His Excellency, Ouyang!

LITERATI FOUNDLING HOSPICES

A detailed description of a Chinese proposal for a foundling hospice is provided by the Jesuit father François-Xavier Dentrecolles in a 1720 letter from Beijing.[12] The hospice was for exposed children and it was to be sponsored by local patrons. Dentrecolles translated several pages from a book entitled *On the Complete Happiness of the People*, which was written by an unidentified Chinese literatus and included this proposal. The proposal described a quasi-official institution in which the local magistrate would use government funds as seed money to initiate the project. The magistrate would recruit the most distinguished local literati and wealthy people, whom he would persuade to support the project with their services and financial contributions.

A man of venerable age and proven character was to be chosen as director (*dongshi*) of the foundling hospice.[13] His term was to be limited to three years, although sometimes there were several directors, and terms were limited to one year. He would reside at the hospice and be in charge of buying supplies and paying salaries. The director would assign low-ranking individuals to collect the exposed children. These collectors would divide the city into segments and make rounds each morning to gather any exposed children and bring them to the hospice by noon. This should involve eight men who would each have a wheelbarrow (tipcart) covered by a canopy. In the winter, the canopy would be fitted with a thick rug to protect the infants from the wind and cold. In the summer it would have a thin linen cloth to shield the infants from the harsh sunlight while allowing for fresh air. Those infants found dead were to be gathered and buried.

Historical records indicate that infants brought to foundling hospices were immediately inscribed in a "register of collected children" (*shou-yingce*).[14] This included, if known, the child's name, date of birth, and physical characteristics. If unknown, the date of birth was estimated. Some hospices also made fingerprints of the child, to be placed on a small card with other information and kept with the child to avoid misidentification when assigned to the wet nurses.

According to Dentrecolles, the model foundling hospice would follow ancient precedent and be located in a healthful and attractive site. The hospice compound would be enclosed by solid walls and a front gate that opened into a courtyard. One large main building would serve for communal affairs, for assemblies, and for greeting visitors. Two wings built in Chinese style on one floor around the courtyard would house offices on one side and food supplies on the other. Thirty rooms would be devoted to housing the wet nurses who would be accommodated three to a room. At the end of these lodgings there would be a garden to temper the scorching summer heat and to serve as a drying place for washed linen and clothing. The wet nurses would be carefully selected and require a guarantor. The proposal reflected some awareness of the practical needs and problems in running such an institution. Perhaps the most crucial factor in securing the survival of these infants involved the quality of the wet nurses. Because the wet nurses had no maternal bonds to the children they were caring for, the proposal recognized that care in the nurses' selection and adequate compensation for their work were essential. The terms for "wet nurse" (*nai mu* and *rumu*) used in Qing medical texts were identical to those of "nursing mother" and made no assumption that the nursing woman was the biological mother.[15]

Each wet nurse was to receive food, lodging, and wages. In Dentrecolles' proposal, each wet nurse would receive thirty measures of rice each lunar month (twenty-nine and one-half days), with one measure of rice being sufficient for one day's nourishment. In historically documented cases, wet nurses were paid a monthly salary of three *qian* (0.3 tael) of silver, which would buy eighteen catties (*jin*) of rice (one catty = 0.5 kg).[16]

The building that housed the wet nurses was to have a front and back gate, both carefully guarded by two matrons who were to be well paid and who would carefully guard against unauthorized entries. Men were usually excluded, although some hospices allowed a wet nurse's husband to live in her room. Every third day the steward would inspect the children and if he found any poorly cared-for children, he would admonish the responsible wet nurse. If the children fell ill, a physician would come to treat them.

The funding of the foundling hospice would be the responsibility of prominent local literati and wealthy people who would act as trustees. These would be twelve in number, in order to allow for a one-month rotation of each trustee. During his month of supervisory activity, each trustee would reside at the hospice. One day each month the trustees would gather for a business meeting. Three days before this meeting the director would send out an announcement of the meeting date and would send bills of expenses. A modest meal would be served prior to the meeting. The proposal emphasized that expenditures for food and drink should be limited in order to prevent socializing and convivial detraction from the meeting's business purpose. Nevertheless, in a concession, the proposal allowed that during cold weather, three cups of wine per person would be permitted.

At each meeting, a financial report compiled by the director and current supervising trustee was presented. The report would include a list of each donor and the amount of the contributions. In addition, it would include the number of exposed children who had been collected, the number of children who had died, the current number of employees, and whether the benefactors' contributions had been in money or provisions.

The Chinese literatus who formulated this proposal only briefly mentioned that a great many more girls than boys were abandoned. In fact, the hospice would be filled predominantly with girls. There were many requests from outsiders to take these girls and raise them. In order to give these requests the necessary scrutiny, administrators set aside one day each month to consider them. The supervising trustee and steward were to investigate the character and profession of the person making the request; the purpose of this investigation was to eliminate those who wished to take the girls in order to sell them for a profit. Some of the girls were sought as brides, even though they could offer no dowry to the groom. The arrangement seems to have been like a minor marriage (*tongyangxi*).

Minor marriages involved the betrothal of a child and her immediate transfer to the household of a future husband. Because of the frequent sex-ratio imbalance, girls were in short supply and a young girl of marriageable age could command a high bride-price. Peasants unable to afford the bride-price would buy an abandoned girl. In some areas minor marriages became more common than raising a birth daughter.[17] The adopting family acquired the services of a maid as the girl was assimilated into the family.[18] The family compensated for the girl's lack of a dowry by avoiding the cost of a go-between and an expensive marriage feast. Adopting a little daughter-in-law in a minor marriage cost as little as a chicken and a bottle of wine. The betrothal was binding and the son was guaranteed a wife. Although the girl might suffer a fate of being overworked or treated cruelly by her future mother-in-law, she had a secure place in her adoptive family. A minor marriage probably would have been the best fate that a girl in a foundling hospice could hope for; many girls instead probably ended up as permanent maids or concubines, but at least even these arrangements would allow them to avoid prostitution or more abusive forms of existence.

The proposal described by Dentrecolles was a model foundling hospice rather than a description of a particular institution. The quality of foundling hospices in China appears to have varied by time and place, depending on the fluctuating levels of financial support from the state and private individuals. The Jesuit Maurice du Baudory (Zhang Maoli), who ministered to abandoned children in Canton in the early eighteenth century, described the government-run orphanage there in exemplary terms.[19] He claimed it was large and magnificent, with everything needed to maintain these foundlings, including wet nurses to feed them, physicians to treat their illnesses, and administrators to make sure everything functioned smoothly. By contrast, in 1844, Monsignor Rizzolati described the government-run foundling hospice in Wuchang in dire terms. He claimed that children quickly died of hunger there because corrupt administrators assigned each wet nurse the impossible task of feeding five, six, or even seven children at a time. Additional information about the condition of this Canton foundling hospice in 1844 comes from the missionary George Smith. On a visit to Canton he was told by his former Chinese tutor, Choo, that this Canton institution, which was located in the eastern suburbs of Canton, about one mile outside of the city, was the only government-sponsored foundling hospice in Guangdong Province. It was said to have been supported in the past by fees levied on ships trading at Canton. The implication was that the abolition of the Canton system of trade by the Opium War and Treaty of Nanjing (1842) had disrupted the flow of funds to the institution. Choo claimed that the foundling hospice took in five thousand girls each year, though it was able to house only one thousand at any given time. Each child remained in the hospice for only two to three months before being sent to a wet nurse to be cared for or before being taken to a wealthy merchant or gentry home to be raised as a future concubine or servant.[20]

In the eighteenth century, many hospices had more than one hundred rooms and some of the largest, such as Jiangdu in the prefecture of Yangzhou, had four hundred rooms at its peak. The administration of the hospices began to deteriorate in the second half of the eighteenth century. The ideal principles of having one wet nurse per child and requiring that wet nurses reside at the hospice had to be abandoned in the face of the crushing increase in orphans. The Tongzhou gazetteer of 1755 indicates that in the years 1664–1755, the hospice gathered sixty thousand abandoned children, even though the recorded population of Tongzhou in 1711 was only 69,277.[21] The quality of orphanages declined in the reign of the Daoguang emperor (1821–1850). Poor management of the hospices and other factors produced mortality rates that commonly reached 50 percent. The mortality rates grew so high that in 1845 a salt merchant and scholar of Yangzhou punned on the name of foundling hospices, calling them "infanticide hospices" (*shaying tang*).[22]

Nevertheless, philanthropic efforts continued. The problem of poor people in remote areas being unable to bring their infants to the hospices was recognized. In the early eighteenth century, holding stations were established in remote areas in order to collect children for sending them on to urban orphanages. These were called "receiving halls for infants" (*jieying tang*) or "retaining halls for infants" (*liuying tang*).[23] The network of these charitable institutions continued to expand, particularly in the Lower Yangzi area until the Taiping Rebellion (1850–1864) destroyed the movement's momentum.

CONFUCIAN ARGUMENTS AGAINST FEMALE INFANTICIDE

Qing literati attempts to combat infanticide took the form of official proclamations banning the practice, publicly circulated essays condemning the practice (*jieninü wen*), participation in protection societies, and contributions of money, food, and supplies to foundling hospices (*yuying tang*). These efforts reflected the high culture of Confucian values and differed from the popular culture of the morality books (*shan shu*) with their syncretic blending of Confucianism, Buddhism, and Daoism. The literati efforts were marked by a far greater emphasis on rationality and social responsibility and imbued with the patronizing spirit of class superiority. The imaginative and sometimes supernatural stories so favored by the general populace were less a part of the literati efforts. Because officials were also Confucian scholars, the government often supported these literati efforts, mixing public welfare with private charity. Nevertheless, all of these efforts had limited effectiveness in stopping infanticide.

Palatre's collection of Chinese documents begins with the supposedly earliest Qing imperial edict dealing with infanticide. This was a 1659 petition by the official Wei Yijie (1616–1686) to the first Qing ruler, the Shunzhi emperor.[24] Wei Yijie had been appointed to the elevated position of president of the Censorate (the highest oversight agency) only two years before. He was a follower of the orthodox Neo-Confucian philosopher Zhu Xi, but was also very sympathetic to Christianity. In his testimonial on the seventieth birthday of the Jesuit missionary Adam Schall (1661), Wei made positive comparisons between Confucianism and Christianity and may even have been a secret Christian. His petition was harshly critical of the drowning of little girls that he heard was commonplace in the southeastern provinces of Jiangsu, Anhui, Jiangxi, and Fujian. The Shunzhi emperor approved Wei's petition and with the assistance of the officials Wang Xi and Cao Benrong, issued an edict against infanticide. The edict quoted the famous passage from *Mencius* 2A.6: "If people today see a child on the verge of falling into a well, they will all feel fear and anxiety." This passage has traditionally been used to argue for the innate goodness of human beings, a goodness that implied that drowning little girls was unnatural.

One of the Confucian themes reiterated in the official documents was the balancing of pairs in nature's creation, such as the forces of heaven and earth, yang and yin, and males and females. This theme appeared in an official warning against female infanticide that was affixed to the walls throughout Shanghai in 1866. The drowning of girls was condemned because it "causes extreme harm to the Heavenly Principle (*Tianli*)" and "violates heavenly harmony (*Tianhe*)."[25] The warning used the metaphor of the tiger and the wolf, which, even though they were voracious animals, did not devour their young. The message was that humans should be at least as humane toward their children as these beasts were toward their offspring. This tiger metaphor appeared repeatedly in the literature condemning female infanticide.

The argument of cosmic balance was made in an 1873 proclamation by Governor-General Ling of Huguang (a Ming-dynasty province divided during the Qing dynasty into Hubei and Hunan provinces). He argued that the number of sons and daughters the population produced depended on heaven's determinations, which should not be impeded through infanticide. Ling's proclamation also raised the practical concern that while many poor men were unable to find a wife, it was unheard of for a girl not to find a husband. This situation had been a problem in this area for some time. A European missionary noted in Hubei in 1847 that the great number of infanticides, especially in the neighboring province of Hunan, had produced a shortage of women in that area. This had given rise to an illegal and secret "large commerce of little girls from other provinces."[26]

Female infanticide was sometimes linked to the broader topic of abusive treatment of women. This link was voiced through the wheels of bureaucracy in an 1815 petition to the throne by a literatus named Wu Xingqing of Wuyuan in Anhui Province.[27] Wu complained that the people of Wuyuan were violating Confucian morality by engaging in selling daughters (*yuqi*), drowning girls (*ninü*), and divorcing their wives without regard to the Seven Grounds for Divorce (*qichu zhi tiao*). These Seven Grounds were: failure to beget a son, adultery, disobedience to a husband's parents, a bitter tongue, stealing, envy, and any evil disease.

Wu complained that this treatment of women was a violation of the Confucian Five Relationships (ruler-subject, parent-child, husband-wife, elder-younger, and friend-friend). He claimed that because the drowning or selling of a daughter estranged those from their proper roles involving care and love in the parent-child relationship, this evil custom should be prohibited. The Jiaqing emperor responded promptly and favorably by sending an imperial edict to the governor of Zhejiang Province, Zhang Boling (1748–1816), who, in turn, issued an official proclamation in 1816 prohibiting these practices.

The models of famous filial daughters were cited by literati as a reason for preserving the lives of little girls. Governor-General Ling's proclamation of 1873 prohibiting female infanticide cited the legendary examples of the daughters Ti Ying and Mulan.[28] Ti Ying's father, Chunyun Yi (b. 205 BC), was a Han dynasty official with no sons and five daughters. When he was condemned to dismemberment by the emperor, he cursed his lack of sons who might have assisted him. Ti Ying (ca. 157 BC), the youngest of his daughters, was so deeply affected by her father's outburst that she went to the emperor, offering to become a slave in order to save her father. The emperor was so moved by her willingness to sacrifice herself that he pardoned her father from his punishment.

The second example was Hua Mulan of the Liang dynasty (ca. 501–556), whose modern feminist connotations made her the subject of the 1998 Walt Disney animated film *Mulan*. According to legend, when Mulan's father was recalled to military duty on the frontier, he was ill and unable to go but had no sons to take his place. To save her father from the consequences of disobeying an order, Mulan put on his military outfit and impersonated him as a soldier. For twelve years she served in his place without revealing that she was a woman.

Officials attempted to limit dowries because of their connection to female infanticide. Weddings typically involved formal betrothals with a contract signed by the parents or guardians. In addition, the wedding gifts of the bride's family had to be acceptable to the groom's family for the wedding to occur. The entire collection of wedding gifts to the groom's family formed the dowry, or bride's trousseau (*zhuanglian* or *jiazhuang*). Most of these were contributed by the bride's family, although others might add to the collection.[29] Families often went into debt in order to enhance their daughter's dowry, yet customs of doing this varied by region in China. In Beijing in the early twentieth century, a bride's dowry often included all the furniture and items needed for a household, including even servant girls.

In 1879 Governor Cheng of Zhejiang Province issued a proclamation that criticized dowries as the cause of female infanticide:

> The main cause of this crime comes from the excessive amount spent on marriages. I have learned that among the people a man does not marry a girl without making extensive preparations. The costs sometimes rise from one hundred to one thousand taels of silver; the smallest sum expended amounts to several hundred or dozens of taels; and, in order to procure such sums, property is sold and loans are contracted. The family of the bride regards it as a mark of honor to expend large amounts on behalf of the wife, and there is a lack of stinginess. Moreover, the father-in-law and mother-in-law of the new bride measure the hate or love that they will show to her, on the importance or the scantiness of her dowry. After the marriage, there are still the different periods of three, seven, and fourteen days and a lunar month, during which the family of the spouse should offer presents to the relatives of the husband. If these presents are costlier, they are received with more honor; if they are only of mediocre value, they will be laughed at. The same custom also applies for the new year and the different seasons. Before the birth of a child, swaddling clothes and food are offered. After the child's birth, from the [third day] when he has been washed and his head shaved down to the completion of his first year, it is also necessary to give new presents of food and clothes. The same thing is repeated when he attains the age of ten years, and the amount expended becomes incalculable. Nevertheless, the family of the bridegroom and the wife herself testify to their discontent, if they receive inconsiderable offerings. That is a truly senseless custom. To recognize the obligations of marriage and yet only to be occupied with wealth, these are abuses against which the ancients have protested.[30]

In spite of official attempts to discourage extravagant dowries, the custom was so ingrained in Chinese society that these efforts had little effect.

NINETEENTH-CENTURY INFANT PROTECTION SOCIETIES

In the mid-nineteenth century in the Lower Yangzi River region there was a creative movement to organize infant protection societies (*baoying hui*). A literatus and member of the gentry named Yu Zhi (1809–1874) led this movement. Although Yu attained only the lowest academic degree of *xiucai*, he distinguished himself as a scholar in compiling works like the *Deyi lu* and in his philanthropic leadership as a charitable person.[31] A local history of his native town, Wuxi, listed him under the category of "righteous men" (*xingyi*). He was particularly concerned about unwanted girls, and in 1842 he raised contributions among his fellow gentry in Wuxi to establish an infant protection society. He organized similar societies in neighboring Jiangyin in 1848 and, after the disruption of the Taiping Rebellion, in Huzhou in 1870 and Songjiang in 1874. The funds would come from the local gentry who would make monthly contributions of either rice or 360 copper cash per share.[32] Support was given to needy mothers and newborn infants who lived within ten kilometers (six miles) from the village. One peck (approximately ten liters) of rice and two hundred copper cash would be contributed each month for the first five months of the child's life, after which the child might be sent to a foundling hospice. It was hoped that this support would save the child from being killed.

In the late nineteenth century, female infanticide accelerated in the central and southern parts of China where the Taiping Rebellion had caused great social and economic upheaval. The decline in population was so severe that many gentry became concerned. Since an expanding populace was linked in many minds to prosperity, infanticide became viewed as a threat to China's well-being. The book *The Misfortunes of Jiangnan* speaks of the post-Taiping famine that caused parents to drown newborn boys as well as girls (fig. 3.1) and to abandon many older children.[33] This was confirmed by several official proclamations.

A proclamation in 1867 by Acting Provincial Administration Commissioner Wang of Jiangsu Province expressed concern over the worsening of conditions since the Taiping Rebellion and the increase in female infanticide. The practice had expanded from poor families to affluent families and even included the drowning of second sons.[34] Wang claimed that the reason for this was the lack of foundling hospices and the dissolution of the former infant protection associations in this region. Wang's concern was echoed by other officials in the Lower Yangzi River region. Governor Yang of Zhejiang Province spoke of the need to reestablish orphanages and protection associations that had been destroyed by the Taiping Rebellion in order to deal with this "evil practice of drowning girls."[35]

A second factor—Chinese anxiety over foreign-missionary foundling homes—may have played an even greater role in reestablishing protective institutions than did compassion for suffering children[36:] Chinese gentry supported child welfare in order to help fight Western imperialism. Yang expressed a concern about foreigners (*yangren*) establishing orphanages and feeding Chinese children. In 1872 Shen Bing, an official in Shanghai, petitioned the governor-general, Zhang Sushang of Liangjiang (Jiangsu and Anhui provinces), with a warning about how infanticide was allowing foreigners to displace the Chinese in establishing orphanages.[37] Shen

Figure 3.1.　Famine in the wake of the Taiping Rebellion (1850–1864) caused parents to drown newborn girls by throwing them into the lakes and streams. *Jiangnan tielei tu xinbian* (Suzhou, no date), reproduced in Palatre, *L'infanticide*, p. 84.

believed that foreigners had the ulterior motive of gathering Chinese children for transport to foreign countries, and he referred to suspicious foreign activities of this nature in Yangzhou and Tianjin in previous years.

Shen was referring to the Tianjin Incident of 1870, one of the worst anti-Christian outbursts in the nineteenth century.[38] In the Arrow War (1856–1860), Anglo-French forces landed at Tianjin and marched to Beijing. Foreign troops were stationed at Tianjin from 1858 to 1865, and in 1860 the French appropriated the imperial villa in Tianjin as a consulate. By the terms of the treaties of Tianjin (1858) and Beijing (1860), ten additional Chinese ports were forcibly opened for trade and missionary activities. Using these treaties in 1869 as their legal justification, Catholic missionaries under French protection built the Church of Our Lady of Victories on the site of a razed Buddhist temple in Tianjin, and the French Sisters of Charity established an orphanage there.

The nuns engaged in the typical practice of gathering and baptizing abandoned children, but many of these children were moribund and died soon after entering the orphanage. When thirty-four of the collected orphans died in an epidemic, wild rumors circulated that the Sisters of Charity were using the dead children's eyes and hearts to make medicine. Palatre added a footnote to elaborate on Shen's suspicions in this regard, noting that in addition to the charge of large-scale kidnapping against missionaries, many Chinese believed that the missionaries wanted to dismember the children and mix their hearts, eyes, and brains with opium to make a medicine that could be sold for a financial profit.

These events in Tianjin provoked in the Chinese a virulent antiforeign feeling toward the French. Chinese resentment was further inflamed by the nuns' well-intended but naive offer of payment to those bringing children to the orphanage. This offer unfortunately gave rise to rumors of the kidnapping of children by unscrupulous child brokers. When a Chinese servant of the church was accused of kidnapping children, Chinese authorities investigated. In June 1870, the French consul Henri Fontanier went to the yamen of Chonghou, the leading Chinese official in Tianjin, and confronted him about this investigation. Fontanier irresponsibly drew his pistol and shot wildly at Chonghou, missing him but killing his servant. Fontanier then recklessly confronted the enraged mob of several thousand Chinese who had gathered outside of the official's office. The mob hacked Fontanier and his assistant to pieces.

The mob then went on a rampage, killing and savagely mutilating every French person they could find. Catholic nuns were stripped naked and violated. Their eyes were gouged out, their breasts were cut off, and they were burned alive. In all, twenty-one foreigners (including two French officials, ten nuns, and two priests) were killed. In addition, between thirty and forty Chinese converts were killed. In the melee, the

French consulate, church, and orphanage were plundered and burned to the ground.[39] Four English and American chapels were also destroyed. A number of children died in the burning of the orphanage.

Shen Bing worried that the decline in births since the Taiping Rebellion along with infanticide was impeding the regeneration of the population. His concern over population decline was shared by many literati and officials. In 1874 Shen, having become the *Daotai* of coastal defense in Shanghai, sent another petition to the governor of Jiangsu and Anhui provinces, requesting him to protect the little girls by establishing a central orphanage at Shanghai.[40]

Governor Zhang was not entirely sympathetic to Shen's petition. He believed that having infant protection societies pay individual subsidies to the nursing mothers would do far more to save these children than would establishing orphanages.[41] Perhaps he had been influenced by Yu Zhi's proposal for giving monthly stipends to the mothers of unwanted infants. Zhang claimed that if these steps were taken, "abandoned newborn girls would no longer be seen on seacoasts and riverbeds and on the roadside and the foreigners (*wairen*) would no longer be able to chatter and make an ostentatious display of their charity."

Shen was apparently assigned to deal with the problem of female infanticide. As maritime subprefect of Songjiang and head of the Shanghai office of the Bureau for Infant Protection (*Baoying ju*), he issued a proclamation dated October 27, 1875, that was affixed to the walls of Shanghai.[42] Branch offices of this agency were established, advised by local elders, and authorized to dispense money, clothing, and other necessities to families in an effort to prevent infanticide.

Palatre's collection of documents shows how during the two centuries between 1659 and 1878, the Chinese government encouraged local gentry (landowners and unemployed scholar-officials) to organize and contribute financially to such societies. There was a complex and symbiotic relationship between the government and local gentry. The main purpose of the societies was to assist poor families and prevent them from killing their unwanted baby girls. Sometimes the government would have the quasi-official Bureau for Infant Protection perform official functions for the protection societies. Sometimes the government took the initiative in organizing such societies.

This Bureau for Infant Protection formulated thirty-two regulations. The regulations stated that protection societies should disseminate clear and simple prohibitions on the drowning of little girls. When the officials visited the rural areas of their districts each spring and fall, they were obliged to carry the announcement in an official procession, preceded by a runner beating a gong. Officials were supposed to announce to each family that neighbors and local constables (*dibao*) who failed to report cases of infanticide would be subject to the same punishment as those who committed the acts. Informers were supposed to receive a reward of two thousand copper cash (equivalent to approximately two ounces of silver).

The regulations of the protection societies involved oversight of midwives (*wenpo*), many of whom collaborated in the infanticides.[43] Each local constable was responsible for submitting to the subprefect a list of all midwives in his jurisdiction. Each of the midwives would then be licensed and required to oppose any attempt to kill a newborn child. In addition, the midwives were to denounce such perpetrators to the protection society and receive a reward of two hundred or two thousand copper cash, depending on the severity of the offense. Any midwife who assisted in drowning the child or harming it in any other way was to be severely punished.

When an accusation of infanticide came to a magistrate's attention, he was supposed to ask the leaders of the protection society to investigate and supply him with a report before he administered justice.[44] Because the protection societies were established mainly to help poor people, the wealthy were to be treated differently. The society was responsible for making an inquiry into any incident where a wealthy family was accused of infanticide. If found guilty, the family was to be assessed a fine in proportion to its wealth. The fines were to be paid into the treasury of the society, and those who refused to pay were to be prosecuted by the officials.

The Qing dynasty criminal code, *Da Qing lü li*, issued in 1647, was based on the Ming code of laws established by the Yongle emperor (r. 1403–1424) and later modified to include Manchu law. Section 294 declared that anyone who killed his son, grandson, or slave and attributed the crime to another person would be punished with seventy blows of a heavy bamboo and a year and a half of banishment from his home province.[45] Section 319, Article 2 declared that if a parent or grandparent, in the course of punishing his son, daughter, grandson, or granddaughter for disobedience, caused the child's death, he would be punished with a hundred blows of a heavy cane. However, because infants could not express disobedience, the criminal code did not clearly apply to them. In 1772 Ouyang Yong, the surveillance commissioner of Jiangxi Province, submitted a petition on infanticide to the Qianlong emperor. The petition was approved and issued as an imperial edict in 1773.[46] This edict closed the loophole in the Qing legal code by prescribing sixty blows of the bamboo and one year of exile from one's home province for anyone who murdered with premeditation one's child or grandchild.

The list of punishments included in the protective society's thirty-two regulations was more detailed than the Qing legal code. According to these regulations, anyone guilty of a first occurrence of infanticide would be placed in a small cangue with a small yellow flag carrying the inscription "A warning to those who drown their little girls" (*ninü shizhong*). Each day at the sound of the gong the guilty one would be led by an iron chain through the streets of the city and released after one month without a beating. A second offense was to incur wearing a large cangue at the entryway to the magistrate's tribunal. After three months, the guilty party was to be whipped and released. A third offense incurred the punishment prescribed by law: sixty blows of the bamboo and one year of exile from one's home province. A midwife who killed a newborn child was to be punished by strangulation. Those who aided or had knowledge of infanticide and did not try to prevent it, whether servants, midwives, neighbors, parents, or local constables, were to be similarly punished as accomplices. These prescribed punishments, in spite of (or perhaps because of) their elaborate detail, appear to have been wish lists of justice that were rarely enforced. The presence in proclamations of the official admonition "Do not regard this as a mere formal document that will not be implemented" (*shi wei juwen*) may be more than just conventional official phrasing.[47] It may indicate that the proclamations banning infanticide were not being taken seriously by the people.

The thirty-two regulations of the protection societies also specified that the trustees of the township organization (*dudong*) should become acquainted with the poorest families in the countryside and enter the names of pregnant women and their husbands and the condition of their houses into a register. The birth of their children should be announced and the women should receive financial aid. However, if within the space of ten lunar months the protection society was not informed of the birth of a child, the presumption of a miscarriage or infanticide should cause men to be dispatched to gather information. The district elders (*qudong*) should send a report to the protection society office and if a crime had occurred, punishment should be administered. In spite of their charitable intentions, the protection societies were forced to limit their assistance. The drowning of girls was so extensive that the societies sometimes were forced to restrict their support to healthy little boys.

Another Chinese author lamented in 1869 how widespread the drowning of girls had become and noted that the custom had become so ingrained in China that it no longer evoked outrage.[48] In fact, jokes were made about how infanticide gave girls a chance to be reborn as boys. One gruesome variation of this chance for rebirth was reported in 1876 in the Shanghai newspaper *Minbao*:

> In Huizhou Prefecture in Guangdong Province there exists a very evil custom. When a woman gives birth to a little girl, because the child will cause expense, impoverishment of the family, and difficulties at the time of marriage, it is tipped headfirst into a vase of wine that is called the *beverage of*

transmigration. It is thus suffocated by intoxication, in order that it may return to the palace of Yanluo, king of hell, in order to return later to earth in another baby. This little girl at birth had only a breath of life, so she was incapable of assimilating a similar quantity of wine, and she died of suffocation. Immediately she is taken and thrown into the river.[49]

The author complained that infanticide had become so ordinary that rather than being renounced, it was on the increase. The writer knew of one extended family that had drowned more than ten little girls in one year. Foundling hospices established in the cities in order to give refuge to the unwanted children were too far away from the poor peasants in the countryside for whom even the small expense involved in such a journey would have been prohibitive.

The Confucian tradition laid great stress on model emulation as a way of influencing people. Examples of outstanding men and women were praised and presented as models for others. This pattern was applied to fighting female infanticide in an 1877 petition to the Guangxu emperor by Liu Bingzhang, the governor of Jiangsu Province. It involved the exemplary behavior of Shen Yanqing, the former subprefect of Poyang.[50] Liu requested the emperor to order the Historiographical Institute to enter Shen's name in the "upright officials" (*xunli*) biographies section of the dynastic history. Shen had distinguished himself by his zeal in prohibiting infanticide, in helping the people at the time of flooding, and for his glorious death on the battlefield while fighting the Taiping rebels. In addition, he had established orphanages and organized assistance for unwanted girls.

In describing the Chinese organized efforts to combat infanticide, Palatre gave the impression that the situation in the late nineteenth century was deteriorating. But several scholars have argued that the post-Taiping organizers were becoming more effective in treating infanticide by shifting from supporting costly foundling hospices to giving aid directly to the families of abandoned children.[51] This new approach complemented the growth of Chinese institutions for "preserving women's chastity" (*baojie*). These institutions provided direct aid to widows so that they would not be forced to remarry in order to survive and so could preserve their fidelity to a deceased husband.

4

✛

Infanticide Deniers

DENIAL IN HISTORY

Repeatedly in history, large segments of a population refuse to accept certain traumatic events as factual. The horror of such events in terms of the brutality and large number of victims arouses a certain degree of skepticism about whether events happened in the dimensions claimed. In itself, the skepticism is reasonable, but when continued in the face of a growing body of evidence, it becomes a form of denial.

To what extent the phenomenon of mass denial about female infanticide applies to the Chinese themselves is difficult to say because Chinese religious and moral values did not see the beginning of life in the same way as Westerners. Moreover, Buddhist transmigration provided an ameliorating factor in rebirth that Christianity does not offer. In the Confucian system of values, age—not youth—was venerated. To Chinese moralists, female infanticide was a crime, but not as horrifying a crime as it was to Christians. It is this Christian horror of female infanticide that defines a particular category of deniers who were primarily foreign (European and American).

Infanticide deniers have often been motivated by sympathy for the Chinese, which led them to defend the Chinese against the accusation of killing infants. The problem is that sympathy can be just as much of an obstacle to facing the truth as hatred of a group (i.e., xenophobia). While nineteenth-century Protestant missionaries were notorious for their insensitive views of Chinese culture as backward and superstitious, this contempt was mixed with sympathy for the Chinese people on a human level. This is clearly seen in certain Protestant missionaries who regarded these horrible accusations of female infanticide as being unfair to the Chinese they knew and clearly liked. By contrast, the nineteenth-century Catholic missionaries, and particularly the French Jesuits, were far more critical of the Chinese and yet they had a more realistic understanding of the extent of infanticide in China than did their Protestant counterparts.

As the nineteenth century advanced and Protestant missionaries learned more about Chinese culture, many of them came to accept the pervasiveness of infanticide. Nevertheless, many foreign observers of the Chinese continued to resist, as is seen in the split vote in a debate on infanticide at an 1885 meeting of the North China Branch of the Royal Asiatic Society. And what is more remarkable is that a classic expression of a Chinese workingwoman's woes and triumphs, *A Daughter of Han*, makes no mention of infanticide.[1] Ida Pruitt (1888–1985), who recorded this oral history of Old Mrs. Ning (Ning Lao Taitai), was the daughter of Southern Baptist China missionaries and very sympathetic to the Chinese. It is difficult to conceive that among all the horrors of poverty and sickness and death and drug addiction that Ning Lao Taitai (1867–after 1938) encountered, she never encountered female infanticide although infanticide was widespread in Shandong Province, where she lived.

Was Ida Pruitt an infanticide denier? Certainly not in terms of vocally denying it, but was she an infanticide denier by her silence? Given her work as head of the Social Services Department at Peking Union Medical College from 1921 to 1939, it is inconceivable that she did not encounter female infanticide. She worked with infants and in her book, *Old Madam Yin*, she describes how her hospital provided an eight-month-old male child for adoption to a wealthy Beijing family.[2] The Peking Union Medical College was founded in 1913 with funding from the Rockefeller Foundation.[3] Its sponsor, John D. Rockefeller, was a devout Baptist and through the board of the Northern Baptists, he was a large contributor to Christian missions. The explanation for denial may lie partly in the tendency among missionaries and mission-related agencies like hospitals to gloss over or omit controversial elements that might have hindered the soliciting of mission support. Whereas Catholics publicized infanticide in China to garner support, Protestants conversely may have omitted discussion of it for the same reason.

Confrontation was alien not only to missionary culture, but also to Chinese culture, which Pruitt absorbed during her long stay in China.[4] She had a classic disagreement with her mother over the imposition of Christianity, cleanliness, and the American way of life on the Chinese and instead followed her father's more accommodating approach. Over the years, she became bicultural, absorbing the Chinese concept of "talking into harmony" (*shuohede*). Far from being an emancipated "new American woman" who sought to reform the Chinese, Pruitt accepted the Chinese as they were, except for seeking to help those in need. This might explain her reluctance to criticize the Chinese for infanticide. In this sense, her attitude was completely at odds with the late nineteenth-century Catholic missionaries.

How does one measure the dimensions of female infanticide in China? Since the evidence is far more qualitative than quantitative, it is difficult to make an estimate. The population of China was 160 million in 1700, 350 million in 1800, 600 million in 1950, and 1.3 billion in 2008. Some demographers disagree with Thomas Malthus and argue that female infanticide played a greater role than famine in limiting population growth in China.[5] However, in the last part of the twentieth century, new medical technology produced a modification in female infanticide. Ultrasound imaging machines created the possibility of sex-selective abortions, which were far more efficient than older methods of infanticide. Projecting from government statistics of a nationwide birth ratio of almost 119 boys for every 100 girls in 2005, it is estimated that an accumulated total of thirty million females in China are missing. Not all of these missing girls died of abortions. Many of them died of abandonment and neglect, and some probably died of old-style infanticide techniques. Most of them did not even have their births reported. Nevertheless, the ultimate results were produced by conscious decisions made by parents and tolerated by Chinese society, even if condemned by the government. To this extent, it represents a continuation of two thousand years of female infanticide in China and involves a dimension measurable in the millions.

The scholarship on female infanticide is still relatively sparse. The lack of women scholars in the past has probably contributed to this neglect, and it is significant that most of the scholars now studying the topic are women.[6] Why has the subject inspired so little interest among scholars? Has the continuation of the tradition of denial also contributed to this neglect? These are difficult questions to answer, but they are important to consider.

PROTESTANT MISSIONARY INFANTICIDE DENIERS

The strong resistance of many nineteenth-century Europeans and Americans to accept infanticide as a widespread phenomenon in China was due partly to a lack of knowledge of the facts. Sometimes the grounds for the denial were trivial, as when the Scottish Protestant missionary and interpreter William C. Milne (1815–1863) doubted the often-mentioned claim that vehicles went through the streets of Beijing early in the morning gathering abandoned infants. Milne, who served as a language teacher in the British Legation in Beijing in 1861–1863, claimed that the streets of Beijing were too narrow to allow vehicles to pass through. The matter is easily resolved by noting that the vehicles were tipcarts bearing the Buddhist inscription "The boat of mercy that ferries people [to the other shore for rebirth]"(*cichuan pudu* or *cihang pudu*).[7] Milne was thinking of horse-drawn vehicles when in fact much smaller tipcarts were used.

Milne's Scottish background is relevant here. In 1690 the Scots' Parliament enacted a statute making infanticide an easily proved capital crime. From 1690 to the law's alteration in 1809, hundreds of women were prosecuted and hanged. The victims were mainly unmarried women guilty of illegitimate births. However, due to changes in the economy (an agricultural revolution) and social attitudes, the prosecutions dwindled and the law was eventually revised. What took place was not a decline in the incidence of infanticide in Scotland, but a denial of its occurrence.[8] In the years between 1762 and 1817, doctors, lawyers, jurors, and even the writer Walter Scott began arguing that women did not really kill their children, in spite of evidence to the contrary. Tories and Whigs joined together to reject the probability that the new rural economy might be responsible for driving women to the desperate and vicious act of killing their children.

At the time of the enactment of the law in 1690, Scottish ministers, lawyers, midwives, and others had been willing to believe evidence accusing women of killing their children and had supported severe punishment. But after 1809 the crime of infanticide was hard to prove, and the trial usually ended in a mild punishment involving whipping and, later, a few months in jail. The underlying facts were that the capitalist transformation of agriculture was destroying the traditional culture and social structure by turning small tenant farmers into transient rural wage laborers. The improvement in agricultural productivity took its toll on village women struggling to conclude a marriage. In the face of the trials and hangings of women for infanticide, prominent men responded not by reforming the social conditions that gave rise to infanticide, but by denying that women really killed their children. They did this by invoking Enlightenment views of women's biological instincts and material nature, which resulted in infanticide denial. This formed the background of Milne's denial of infanticide in Beijing.

Other grounds for infanticide denial in China were more substantive, but also more difficult to evaluate. Many Protestant missionaries tended to deny the pervasiveness of infanticide because they viewed the claim as a slander on the humanity of the Chinese people. Hostility between Protestants and Catholics was mutual and probably contributed to the denial. Many anticlerical Catholics and secularists in Europe regarded accounts of widespread infanticide in China as the exaggerations of Catholic priests calculated to increase financial contributions for their mission work in China.

Protestant missionary reactions to infanticide were initially quite different from Catholic missionary reactions partly because of the Protestants' later arrival and consequent delay in catching up with the Catholics in their understanding of internal conditions in China. In addition, theological differences and other missionary priorities played a role. While some Protestant denominations (mainly Anglicans and Lutherans) accepted the Catholic claim of sacramental grace, namely, that baptism had an intrinsic power to bestow salvation on infants, most Protestants did not. The chief sponsors of Protestant missions in nineteenth- and early twentieth-century China were evangelicals of Great Britain and the United States. These included the interdenominational China Inland Mission (CIM) and London Missionary Society (LMS), as well as Low Church Anglicans of the Church Missionary Society (CMS), American Baptists and Presbyterians, and the Congregational American Board of Commissioners for Foreign Missions (American Board).

For most of these Protestants, exposed infants were merely a tragic aspect of Chinese life and did not represent an opportunity for baptism. The Protestant emphasis on a believer's (i.e., adult's) baptism and on studying the Bible caused these missionaries to devote more of their energy to founding schools and universities. Whereas Catholic concern for baptizing abandoned infants led them to establish orphanages throughout China, Protestants instead placed their emphasis on education and hospitals.[9]

When the first Protestant missionary, Robert Morrison, arrived in Canton in 1807, Catholics had already been there for more than two centuries. Catholic missionaries had an experience of inland regions that Protestants would not acquire until later in the nineteenth century. Although many of the early Protestants were highly educated and intellectual in nature, the fact that their activities were initially confined to the coastal areas meant that their knowledge of Chinese social customs was limited. This lack of knowledge combined with a lack of theological interest in baptizing abandoned infants contributed to their tendency to minimize the extent of infanticide.

The first American Protestant missionary to China, Elijah Coleman Bridgman (1801–1861), arrived in Canton in 1829. With Morrison's help, he founded a monthly magazine titled the *Chinese Repository* in 1832 and managed it until 1847, when another American missionary, Samuel Wells Williams (1812–1884), took over the editorship. The *Chinese Repository* is one of the most important sources of information about the early Protestant missionaries in China, but there is a notable absence of references to infanticide in its pages because the editors were dubious about claims of its extensiveness. In the May 1838 issue there is an English translation of an official proclamation (February 19, 1838) by the "Lieutenant-Governor Ke" of Guangdong Province.[10] Although this proclamation presented infanticide as a serious problem, Bridgman added an editorial note after the translation, questioning how extensive it was.

Later, in the June 1840 issue of the *Chinese Repository*, Bridgman criticized a book by Walter Henry Medhurst Sr., a missionary of the London Missionary Society, for exaggerating the extent of infanticide.[11] Yet both Bridgman and his younger successor Williams were overconfident and underinformed. In response to Medhurst's writing that infanticide was "wholly confined to the female sex," Bridgman naively wrote: "Daughters are not so much 'despised and neglected' as he supposes," and further that the Chinese "are fond of their children; and, so far as our observation has reached, they usually love their daughters as much as they do their sons." Finally, Bridgman argued that the number of female infanticides was not large given "the known law of population that the sexes are equally numerous."

Clearly, Bridgman was unaware of the imbalance in sex ratios in China that certain Chinese officials had already observed. Ping-ti Ho's groundbreaking study of China's population confirmed the existence of striking imbalances of males to females recorded in local histories of numerous provinces in the years 1776–1850. Ho believed these high male ratios were explained by the "truly overwhelming" evidence of female infanticide, although he conceded that the evidence was qualitative rather than quantitative.[12] Moreover, local histories, especially of the southern provinces, in these years contained official prohibitions of infanticide as well as poems lamenting its cruelty.

Bridgman's collaborator S. W. Williams was an ambitious American who had a gift for learning Chinese and Japanese and no hesitation at the age of twenty-seven in criticizing more experienced China hands. In the June 1939 issue of the *Chinese Repository*, Williams harshly criticized a book by Karl Gutzlaff (1803–1851), an adventurous and experienced German missionary who had traveled up and down the coast of China working as a translator. According to Williams, Gutzlaff exaggerated the extent of infanticide in China. Williams's rejection of Gutzlaff's claim was based more on Williams's attitude than on his experience in China, which was fairly meager.

The attitude of nineteenth-century missionaries toward the Chinese was a complicated mix of love and hate, devotion and revulsion. Williams was far from being a Sinophile. He was repelled by the dirty bodies, the exasperating language, and the vile natures of the Chinese, and he claimed that "there really has not been much beauty distributed among the Chinese."[13] Nevertheless, Williams felt called by God to serve them and he shared with Bridgman a striking sympathy for the Chinese, as is revealed in the following statement from his review.

Notwithstanding Mr. Gutzlaff's assurance concerning the prevalence of infanticide, and the countenance his authority gives to the common ideas among foreigners of its extent among the Chinese, we doubt very much whether he does not belie the character of the people, and make them to be worse than they are: we have no space here to give the grounds of our belief, nor does the subject admit of statistical demonstrations. Infanticide no doubt exists to an extent that must shock every feeling mind, but from the loose way in which the authors have stated their observations and opinions, leaving much room for the reader's imagination to fill up the picture, ideas have become current which place the Chinese parents in a light, much worse we think than sober investigation would warrant.[14]

This sympathy for the Chinese was not shared by all nineteenth-century foreign missionaries and scholars in China. Unlike the scholarly Jesuit missionaries who had admired China in the years before 1800, the post-1800 Jesuit missionaries tended to view China negatively in terms of its culture and paganism. This shift in Jesuit attitudes had been stoked by the crushing and humiliating defeats of the Chinese by superior European military technology combined with the simultaneous emergence of a full-blown imperialist mentality in Europe.

As the century progressed, Protestants became more mixed in their views. These opposing views surfaced in 1885 when the North China Branch of the Royal Asiatic Society attempted to ascertain the extent to which infanticide existed in China by inviting written responses to this question from residents throughout the British Empire. These responses were read and followed by discussion at an open meeting of the society on May 14, 1885, in Shanghai, organized and presided over by the distinguished Sinologist and diplomat Herbert A. Giles (1845–1935). Perhaps Giles's yen for controversy was a motive in organizing this meeting. Certainly he was one of the most vehement infanticide deniers, a viewpoint shaped by the intellectual nature of his interests and his isolation from the mundane aspects of Chinese life.

Giles conceded that infanticide might exist in exceptional circumstances such as famine or rebellion, but on the whole he believed "it to be no more practiced in China than in England, France, the United States or elsewhere."[15] Edward Bays Drew (1843–1924), a commissioner of the Chinese Imperial Customs Service, "believed that missionaries, whose hearts were full of the idea of the wickedness of the institutions and customs of the country, were somewhat liable to be led away by prejudice against those institutions and customs because they were not influenced by Christianity." This antimissionary viewpoint appears to have been endorsed by Giles, who inserted the editorial comment "hear, hear" after Drew's statement. The division among foreigners was reflected in the count of nine pro and eight con on the question of whether infanticide was extensive in China.

KNOWLEDGEABLE PROTESTANT MISSIONARY OBSERVERS

While the extent of infanticide in China was debated, its existence was unable to be denied. In the October 1843 issue of the *Chinese Repository*, there appeared a carefully compiled and reasoned report on infanticide in Fujian Province by the American Protestant missionary David Abeel (1804–1846). At this point, missionaries were confined to the coastal areas of the five treaty ports opened by the Treaty of Nanjing (1842). Abeel lived in Amoy (Xiamen) from 1842 to 1845 and traveled to the coastal district of Tongan in Quanzhou Prefecture of southeastern Fujian. He visited forty different towns and villages in Tongan and based on his queries, he computed that an average of 39 percent of females were destroyed at birth. He found that the cause of infanticide was material avarice and that it was as prevalent among the rich as the poor. This was a striking conclusion because it challenged the conventional wisdom that infanticide in China was caused by poverty. Abeel called infanticide among the rich "an act of heartless calculation—a balancing of mere pecuniary profit and loss."[16] Among the methods used to destroy infant girls was placing the child in a little boat with the hope that she might be rescued by someone downstream.

Abeel notes that foundling hospices supported by officials and wealthy men were limited to large cities and were too meager in number and resources to be effective in combating infanticide. The people Abeel spoke with felt that the admonitions against infanticide written by literati were having an effect and that the practice was in decline. However, Abeel notes that such a decline was impossible to confirm. Williams was so impressed by Abeel's report that he later included reference to it in his monumental two-volume work *The Middle Kingdom* (1874). Yet while Williams conceded the existence of infanticide in Fujian, he denied it for the area around Canton and implied that it was not extensive in China as a whole.[17]

In spite of Abeel's report, there was very little interest in infanticide among nineteenth-century Protestant missionaries. This is reflected in the lack of articles on infanticide that appeared in academic journals like the *China Review*, which was produced in Hong Kong. One exception to this was written by Daniel Jerome Macgowan (1814–1893), who initially was a medical missionary of the American Baptist Missionary Union at Ningbo and later served in the Chinese Customs Service. Although the article is titled "Prevalence of Infanticide in China," it deals with other issues, including the historical background of infanticide in China and the cannibalizing of children.[18]

Macgowan lists three main causes of infanticide: superstition, famine, and poverty. By "superstition," he means the belief that the bodies of children possess healing properties. The medicinal benefit was believed to increase with the youth of the body, with fetuses being the most prized of all. This led to the kidnapping and buying of young children and ultimately to infanticide. Macgowan believed that the rich did not practice infanticide, but in this he was mistaken. His limited knowledge of Chinese social customs was reflected in his comments. Nevertheless, he did make some insightful observations regarding the area around Ningbo (south of Shanghai). Although more than 40 percent of female infants were destroyed in Pingyang, which was poor, very few were destroyed in neighboring Wenzhou, where there were many wealthy and educated people. Moreover, the girls in Wenzhou possessed marketable value as concubines, prostitutes, and wives, and this marketable value (from ten or thirty dollars to several hundred dollars per girl) had increased since the introduction of steamship connections to Shanghai. The poor people of Pingyang found it cheaper to purchase girls or widows from Wenzhou than to raise them.

As the nineteenth century progressed and Protestants became more engaged with inland areas of China, their assessments of the extent of infanticide began to converge with those of Catholics. Consequently, some Protestant missionaries began to join Catholics in criticizing the European infanticide deniers although the theological differences with Catholics over the issue of infant baptism remained. Charles Piton was a Protestant missionary who studied at the Basel Mission in Switzerland and was a missionary at Lilong (Lilang) among the Hakkas in southern Guangdong Province for twenty years (1864–1884).[19] Intellectual by nature, he began work on a translation of the Bible combining the Hakka dialect and Chinese characters.

After returning to Europe, Piton published several books, including a short work in French titled *L'infanticide en Chine* (1887), indicating just how knowledgeable he was. His claims that female infanticide was widespread in China were attacked by two infanticide deniers who publicly circulated their views in France. One such denier was Chen Jitong (Tcheng Ki-tong) (1851–1907), a colorful Chinese diplomat in France who had a limited knowledge of China and a boundless self-confidence. He was a native of Fujian who had studied at the French-funded Fuzhou Arsenal. In 1876, when he was twenty-six and still not very educated about China, he was taken to France, where he adopted French mannerisms and lifestyle.[20] He applied his bright mind to learning French and wrote several witty books in that language. The Qing government appointed him military attaché and later chargé d'affaires to the Chinese Legation in Paris. However, he disgraced himself by taking unauthorized loans for his personal use and was recalled to China in 1891. Although his knowledge of such matters was meager, he did not hesitate to claim that the incidence of infanticide was as frequent in Europe as in China. The former French consul in China, G. Eugène Simon, claimed that infanticide was even less frequent in China than in France.[21] Chen and Simon also ridiculed Piton's claim that abandoned infants in China were occasionally eaten by pigs.

Another notable portrayal of infanticide in China was published by the Australian journalist George Ernest Morrison (1862–1920). In 1894 Morrison traveled 1,500 miles up the Yangzi River and then another 1,500 miles overland through southwest China to Burma. He dressed in Chinese clothes and had considerable contact with Chinese. The journey transformed his attitude toward China, a transformation that he described thus: "I went to China possessed with the strong racial antipathy to the Chinese common to my countrymen, but that feeling has long since given way to one of lively sympathy and gratitude."[22]

When he visited the city of Zhaotong in northeastern Yunnan Province, Morrison saw starving conditions that made infanticide "dreadfully common."[23] A missionary told him of a woman mission worker who admitted to suffocating three of her female children within days of their birth. When she gave birth to a fourth girl, her enraged husband grabbed the baby by the legs and threw her against the wall, killing her. Of course, stories like this tend to be passed on because of their horror and are not necessarily representative of widespread experiences. More telling was the claim that both dead and living abandoned children were thrown among the grave mounds of Zhaotong, where they were gnawed by dogs. A Protestant missionary told Morrison that one morning when he was leaving the city by the south gate, he came upon a dog eating a living infant who had been thrown over the wall during the night. The infant's arm was crunched and stripped of flesh and the crying baby soon died. Then, a townsman told Morrison that every morning when he went around the city gathering dead dogs and cats for burial, he always found at least one dead child and sometimes three or four. Because poor people were buried in shallow graves, dogs tended to dig up the corpses and eat them.

While conceding that infanticide existed, Morrison rejected the racist view that it was a distinctly Chinese practice. He wrote: "The prevalent idea with us Westerners appears to be that the murder of their children, especially of their female children, is a kind of national pastime with the Chinese, or, at the best, a national peculiarity."[24] He blamed the exaggerated statements of missionaries for being the source of the idea that infanticide was extensive in China, but then he almost contradicted himself by adding that even missionaries were divided on the extent of infanticide in China. He noted that the subject of infanticide had been discussed by "a legion of writers and observers" who concluded that except in times of famine, the practice was "enormously overstated."

Unfortunately, that concluded the balanced part of Morrison's description of infanticide in China. Like a number of Protestant missionaries, he allowed his sympathy for the Chinese to interfere with his objectivity. He also relied too much on the expert testimony of the scholar H. A. Giles and the diplomat G. Eugène Simon, who were uninformed on this aspect of Chinese culture and who uncautiously trumpeted their views as infanticide deniers. Consequently, Morrison did not stop at plausibly claiming that the crime of infanticide was not—apart from times of famine—proportionately greater in China than in England. Rather, he crossed the line into the implausible by claiming that "the crime of infanticide is less common among the barbarian Chinese than is the crime of foeticide among the highly civilized races of Europe and America." In fact, birth control and abortion in the late nineteenth-century Europe and America were largely unavailable or unreliable.[25] Morrison's claim that there were more abortions in the West than infanticides in China appears to have sprung mainly from his newfound enthusiasm for things Chinese (Sinophilia).

By the end of the nineteenth century, although many Protestant missionaries no longer questioned the extent of infanticide, they continued to differ from Catholic missionaries in seeing infanticide as a crime to be condemned rather than an opportunity for baptism. One of the most widely read observers of Chinese society was the American Arthur H. Smith, who served for twenty-six years as a missionary of the American Board. Smith viewed infanticide in China as a crime caused by poverty and practiced on "an enormous scale," especially in the maritime provinces of the south (Guangdong, Fujian, and Zhejiang).[26] Smith viewed infanticide as part of a broader pattern of abuse of women entrenched in Chinese society. Like the nineteenth-century Catholic missionaries, he was highly critical of traditional Chinese culture and saw Christianity as the only solution for China's reform.

A woman missionary had advantages over her male counterparts in investigating the sensitive matter of infanticide. Some of the most striking firsthand observations on infanticide in late nineteenth-century China were made by the American Baptist missionary Adele M. Fielde (1839–1916). Fielde lived an active life as a feminist, missionary, and biologist. She spent ten years (1873–1883) as a missionary at Swatow (Shantou), where she became fluent enough in the Swatow dialect to speak directly with Chinese women and gain unusual access.[27] Swatow is located on the seacoast at the mouth of the Han River in eastern Guangdong Province, near Fujian. It was first opened to foreign trade by the Treaty of Tianjin (1858). Fielde was an early American feminist and her ministry was devoted to Chinese women, whom she trained in teaching the Bible and then sent as missionaries into houses where only women could gain access. In the process, she formed remarkably close relationships with Chinese women, whose autobiographies she recorded by dictation and incorporated into a book titled *Pagoda Shadows*.

The third chapter of this book, "The Extent of a Great Crime," deals with infanticide with a directness and authority rarely found in the handling of this topic.[28] In her journeys through the countryside around Swatow, Fielde "frequently saw the bodies of dead infants and was told they were thrown away when living, because their parents did not want them." In an effort to learn the extent of infanticide and its comparative rate of mortality between males and females, she wrote to women missionaries in other parts of China and collected statistics. Her compiled figures showed that 160 Chinese women over fifty years of age had given birth to 631 sons and 538 daughters. While nearly 60 percent of the males (366) survived beyond ten years of age, only 38 percent of the females (205) did. The 160 women confessed to killing 158 daughters and no sons. Fielde believed that the total number of infanticides was greater than the number confessed to, either because of guilt or simple loss of memory.

The reports indicate considerable regional variations. The report from Ningbo claimed that although infanticide had previously been common, the government had stopped it when wives became scarce. Whereas numerous cases of infanticide were reported at Fuzhou, Amoy, and Canton, the report from Suzhou claimed that female infants were rarely murdered there because of well-subsidized foundling asylums in the city. Children were gathered in the countryside in baskets "like chickens" in groups of ten or twelve (see fig. 5.2) and brought to the asylums in Suzhou. The foundlings from these asylums provided many poor men with wives and many families with servants for whom husbands were eventually found. One of the asylums provided free clothing for children.

Fielde knew of only two foundling hospices within fifty miles of Swatow, although she admitted that there might be others. At one of these, one to two hundred infant girls were taken in each year. Each child was given out to a wet nurse who was paid four cents a day. After twelve days, the healthy infants were placed in a basket and carried by a peddler who sold them in the surrounding villages. Women could examine the contents of the basket and purchase a daughter-in-law. Fielde described her encounter with one of these peddlers:

> Walking one nightfall near Go Chan, I met a man carrying two large covered hampers at the two ends of a pole over his shoulder. Wailing voices issued from the hampers, and I asked the man to let me look at his burden. He lifted the covers, and I found that his wares consisted of three young infants, lying

on their backs, cold, hungry, and miserable. This baby-peddler had taken six little girls out that morning to sell. He had disposed of only half of his stock and was going home with the remainder. He said he was tired and had yet a long way to go, and that, if I would take the lot, I might have all three of the girls for a dollar.

Although it was rare for children other than newborn infants to be killed, Fielde did describe a father, after the death of the mother, taking his three-month-old daughter to the beach and leaving her until the tide washed her out to sea. She comments:

That the drowning of a three-month's-old girl should excite no more comment than the drowning of a kitten, in a village of three thousand people, is marvelous to anyone who does not know how lightly the lives of Chinese girls are esteemed.

Fielde shared a common missionary belief that the two causes of infanticide were "poverty and superstition." Although a feminist, she was also a Christian missionary and she believed that the acceptance of Christianity would cause child murder to cease. She noted that while non-Christian women showed no shame or guilt for killing their children, Christian women did, and they often tearfully asked her to pray that their crimes might be forgiven. She said that although Christianity did not remove the poverty, it led parents to depend on God, rather than on male descendants, for comfort in the afterlife.

5

✛

The European Cult
of Chinese Children

INFANTICIDE DENIERS IN EUROPE

In a letter of December 9, 1846, from Shanghai, the superior of the first group of returning Jesuits to China, Fr. Claude Gotteland, wrote to a fellow priest in Paris:

> That there are still persons who doubt the existence of infanticide in China does not surprise me. It is characteristic of good souls to believe others incapable of crimes which are completely repugnant to their being, but here at the scene of this barbarism, it is not so unbelievable.[1]

Gotteland often spoke to Chinese Christians about the problem of infanticide and treated it as a common affair in China. However, he referred to the victims as "little children" (*petits enfants*) and made no mention of the fact that most of them were girls. It is hard to believe that Gotteland was unaware of this fact because he was well informed on the other details of infanticide. A midwife told him that at the time of birth the child was submerged in a container of water and drowned. He described the container as a bucket that was also used as a toilet or chamber pot. In short, by 1846 accurate details of infanticide in China were known by the Jesuits and widely disseminated in Europe.

By 1875 France was still reeling from its devastating military defeat by Germany only five years before in the Franco-Prussian War, and the country was dominated by anti-Catholic republicans. In response, the Catholic clergy allied with the upper classes and military forces in a reactionary attempt to restore the monarchy. Fed by this mutual hostility, the government of the Third Republic embarked on a program of secularization in which the state took over many activities previously monopolized by the church. State schools replaced religious schools; religious symbols were removed from law courts; marriage ceremonies, which had previously been religious, became civil; God was deleted from oaths and hospitals were laicized. Anticlerical attacks on the Jesuits were particularly virulent. In 1879 the Jesuits were forbidden to teach, and the following year the Society of Jesus was dissolved. Police entered their thirty-seven houses throughout France and expelled the Jesuits.[2] Yet despite the closure of their houses in France, the Jesuits continued to operate out of Belgium and England. As a consequence of the persecution in France, the Jesuits became embattled and their mentality became defensive.

Francisque Sarcey (1827–1899) was a well-known Parisian drama critic noted for his prolific weekly articles. They appeared in Le XIXe Siècle, one of the most popular conservative and anticlerical daily newspapers of the early years of the Third Republic. On November 30, 1875, the first article in a ten-part series dripping with sarcasm entitled "Les Petits Chinois" (The Little Chinese) appeared. A journalist's mentality shaped Sarcey's view of China, and the large readership of his newspaper gave him an inflated sense of importance to speak with an authority on matters of which he knew little. He was locked in a polemical battle in which he saw Catholic priests of his day (particularly the Jesuits) as a malign force and he felt called to expose their deceptive practices. Consequently, his writings are filled with a virulent anticlericalism that contains more drama than light. Although the Jesuits had their own biases, they were more inclined than Sarcey to cultivate knowledge as a polemical weapon. In this instance, we see a battle between Sarcey's impressionistic and fast-moving polemics and the Jesuits' plodding and detailed scholarship combined with their romanticized concern for the abandoned children of China. Sarcey wrote his attacks from Paris, a cultural center of the world. The Jesuits responded from the remote outskirts of faraway Shanghai, a new city that was only then emerging on the banks of the Whangpoo (Huangpu) River.

Sarcey's ten short articles appeared on the front pages of the Le XIXe Siècle from November 30 to December 19, 1875, and were read by thousands of people. By contrast, the Jesuits' response to these articles appeared almost three years later in a crudely produced bilingual (French-Chinese) work that was published in a very limited autograph edition. Most readers would have found the detailed treatment in L'infanticide et l'oeuvre de la Sainte-Enfance en Chine (Infanticide and the work of the Holy Childhood in China) to make for tedious reading. Yet in contrast to Sarcey's hastily written articles, the Jesuits' painstaking accumulation of

Chinese documents provided the basis for an argument that rebutted Sarcey's claims.

Unfortunately, the effectiveness of the Jesuits' argument was recognized by very few readers in Europe. I have found only one review of this book, a balanced evaluation in a scholarly French journal that recognized not only the complexity of the debate over infanticide in China, but also the validity of the Jesuits' argument.[3] And yet Europeans in China were aware of Palatre's book. At their famous debate on infanticide at the North China Branch of the Royal Asiatic Society meeting in Shanghai in 1885, the physician R. A. Jamieson referred to this book as one of the "best authorities on the question of Infanticide."[4]

Sarcey began his first article on the "Little Chinese" by recalling a childhood experience that occurred shortly before his First Communion and probably before he reached the age of twelve. He and his fellow catechumens had been enrolled in the Society of the Holy Childhood (Société de la Sainte-Enfance) and were contributing one sou a month (or week if they were more affluent) to the faraway and exotic little Chinese. A *sou* might amount to approximately one U.S. dollar in today's currency.[5] The plight of the Chinese was romanticized with colorful children's drawings and musical games. Sarcey remembers the priest dividing the children into two groups, one representing the Little Chinese and the other the Holy Childhood children. One group was placed to the right and the other to the left. Then they began singing a song in alternating chorus. First the Holy Childhood group sang:

> Little Chinese, in your need
> We want to help you all
> We will tell our mothers
> Sweet brothers, we will comfort you
> Sweet brothers, we will comfort you

The Little Chinese group responded singing:

> Sweet brothers, help us
> Sweet brothers, help us!

Then both groups in unison sang:

> Sweet brothers, help us
> Sweet brothers, we will comfort you!

Then the group on the right passed to the left and the group on the left passed to the right as the groups changed places and repeated the verses.

Following the canticle, Sarcey remembered colorful images that were often distributed to the children. One in particular was still vivid in his mind.
It depicted a terrible massacre in China. One line was drawn in a beautiful
yellow ochre to represent the Yellow River. Multitudes of children
swarmed on the banks of this river while pigs ran among them, violently
devouring them.[6] This image portrayed one of the most powerful claims
of the Holy Childhood, namely, that because of the poverty in China, abandoned children were being eaten by pigs and dogs. Many years later
Sarcey came to regard these stories as gross exaggerations created to solicit
funds for the mission, and furthermore, he claimed many of the funds collected for this purpose were not even used for Chinese children.

THE HOLY CHILDHOOD AND THE CULT OF THE CHILD

The organization behind Sarcey's childhood meeting had been founded
by Charles de Forbin-Janson (1785–1844). He was born in Paris as a child
of privilege and, like many other Europeans, became inspired by faraway
China. He was a headstrong young man who spurned his noble family's
plans for his marriage by entering the Saint-Sulpice seminary in 1808. He
was diverted from his original intention of going to China by Pope Pius
VII, who urged him to help re-Christianize a France that had been secu-
larized by the French Revolution. He was consecrated bishop of Nancy
and was a zealous preacher but a poor administrator who alienated his
clergy. As an intense royalist, he was forced to flee France after republican
forces removed King Charles X in 1830. In 1839 he went to Rome and
asked Pope Gregory XVI's permission go to China as a missionary, but
was sent to North America instead. In 1839–1841, Forbin-Janson made a
missionary tour of the United States and Canada, where he preached in a
number of cities and evangelized Native Americans.

By 1837 Forbin-Janson had become aware of the practice of infanticide
in China and in 1843 he founded the Society of the Holy Childhood
(sometimes translated as "Association of the Holy Infancy") to save children.[7] His plans to go to China were never realized because in 1844 he
suddenly died at his family's castle near Marseille while he was prepar-
ing to leave. However, his dream survived him. The inspiration for the society was scriptural. The cover page of the first issues of the Holy Childhood's *Annales* depicted a medallion image of Jesus surrounded by
children of different skin colors (fig. 5.1).[8] Around this image is a quote
from the Gospel of Matthew 19:14: "Let the little children come to me"
(*Laissez venir à moi les petits enfants*). Children held a special place in Jesus's teaching and this was part of the inspiration that drove the Holy
Childhood to save Chinese children from infanticide. It also reinforced the

Figure 5.1. A medallion image of the Society of the Holy Childhood featuring Jesus surrounded by children of different skin colors and inscribed with the quotation from the gospel of Matthew 19:14: "Let the little children come to me." This society was founded with the aim of aiding the "little Chinese" (*petits Chinois*). From the title page of *Annales de l'Oeuvre de la Sainte-Enfance* I (Paris, 1846-49)

imagery of the Christ child in a way that oriented the European sensibility toward the helplessness of children.

The Holy Childhood was founded on the cult of the child. Repeatedly in the history of Christianity, social movements emerged in which the purity of children became a spiritual force. The exalted image of the Madonna rests on the purity of how she conceived the Christ child and gave birth to Jesus. Jesus grounded Christianity in poverty and helplessness when he blessed these qualities in the Sermon on the Mount (Matthew 5:1–10). The helplessness of children is the source of their spiritual purity. In the Middle Ages in Europe, there were several movements led by children, and among these children were youthful miracle-workers. The male children of Bethlehem who had been murdered on Herod's orders (Matthew 2:16)—the Slaughter of the Innocents—are regarded as the first martyrs of the Christian church. Since the fifth century they had been revered on Innocents Day (December 28), when children choose their own child-bishop.

After the failure of the Fourth Crusade to retake Jerusalem, it was believed that the poverty and purity of children would empower them to do what the crusader knights had failed to do. This religious enthusiasm became the basis for the Children's Crusade.[9] Beginning in the Rhineland and lower Lorraine in the spring of 1212, several thousand children aged ten to eighteen followed the boy Nicholas of Cologne over the Alps to Genoa, where the crusade disintegrated and some of the children were enslaved by unscrupulous merchants. Today we tend to evaluate the Children's Crusade as hopelessly naive and focus on the failure of adults to protect these children. However, what we fail to see and take seriously is the spiritual purity of children as a powerful force for good. We do not understand the cult of the child.

The Holy Childhood was an attempt to go over the heads of adults in both China and Europe. Chinese children were in desperate need of help because Chinese parents were abandoning and killing their children. The Holy Childhood attempted to save children by appealing to the children of Europe to contribute their pennies and prayers. A phenomenon of children's movements is that they compensate for their lack of individual power by becoming mass movements, as in the Children's Crusade. So the Holy Childhood effort would succeed only if masses of children made small contributions that would accumulate into large amounts. The inefficiency of gathering pennies from children rather than large contributions from rich adult donors is overcome by the purity of the child donors. Adult patrons give money for reasons that are less pure than children and hence diminish the force of their contribution.

There is, of course, a romanticizing of the child here. The reason the work of the Holy Childhood seems so alien to us today is that we tend to see children as naive rather than pure. We believe they need to be protected from abuse, and this leads us to regard the work of the Holy Childhood as hopelessly romantic and exploitive of children. We see this as a cynical attempt by male priests to manipulate children's sympathy and rob their piggy banks. If the Holy Childhood does not rise to the level of sexual abuse in terms of exploitation, it is at least akin to the Pied Piper of Hamelin in misleading children.

Most China Protestant missionaries from Great Britain and the United States did not share this Catholic sensibility. Nineteenth-century Protestantism was dominated by the image of powerful male leaders rather than weak and helpless children. This Protestant emphasis on strength through God seems to have been reinforced by Social Darwinism. While Catholic missionaries in nineteenth-century China devoted themselves to establishing foundling hospices and orphanages to save the weak, Protestant missionaries established schools and hospitals to foster the strong. Of course, Catholics also ran schools and Protestants also ran orphanages, but these were not the groups' emphases.

Great Britain was the leading world power in the nineteenth century and it sponsored the greatest number of missionaries to China. These missionaries were overwhelmingly Protestant and deeply influenced by the Christian Manliness movement that linked physical and spiritual strength.[10] Many missionaries of the Church Missionary Society (CMS) had attended British private schools, which glorified the virtues of athletics. Physical exercise was linked with hard work, martial abilities, and evangelizing. The theme song of this muscular Christianity movement might well have been "Onward, Christian Soldiers," which was written by Sabine Baring-Gould in 1864. This was an evangelical and Low Church Anglican movement that emphasized faith, the Bible, and piety over the priesthood, sacraments, and ritual. Catholics and Anglo-Catholic ritualists were viewed as effeminate, and Baring-Gould questioned their virility. The muscular Christianity movement generated a homophobia that was reinforced by the tendency of Victorian homosexuals, such as those in the Oxford movement, to embrace Anglo-Catholicism and Catholicism.

American Protestant missionaries shared many of these values with their British counterparts. S. Wells Williams took pride in his muscular strength that was superior to that of the Chinese. These missionaries viewed the weakness and effeminacy of the Chinese as things that could be changed by converting them to muscular Christianity. Protestants saw the queue (male pigtail) not only as a mark of Chinese subservience to the Manchus, who had imposed their hairstyle on Chinese males with their conquest of China in 1644, but also as a mark of subservience to Satan, a hairstyle that effeminized Chinese males and made them weak. Body hair became a part of this religious imagery. Beards were very much in vogue in Britain from the 1850s to the 1880s, particularly for dissenting Protestants and Low Church Anglicans; they derided the beardless faces preferred by Anglo-Catholics as effeminate. Thus the lack of facial hair among the Chinese also marked them as effeminate, but since the Chinese tended to have naturally wispy beards, the derision was tinged with racism. Moreover, Chinese men did not grow beards until they reached an advanced age whereas European missionaries of all ages in China, both Protestant and Catholic, tended to grow beards.[11]

During its early years, the Holy Childhood was nicknamed the "Society of the Little Chinese" because its activities were so concentrated on China and surrounding regions. One of the most famous members of the Holy Childhood was the young Chinese martyr Paul Chen Changping

(1838–1861).[12] Chen was born in Guizhou Province into an unstable family. When he was very young, his father abandoned the family over an argument and when he later returned, he found that Chen's mother had remarried. The father took young Chen but, unable to feed him, gave him to a Chinese Catholic priest who raised and educated the boy using funds from the Holy Childhood. Chen's father returned and tried to remove him from the Catholic school, but Chen was determined to finish his studies. In 1860 Chen entered training for the priesthood, but in the following year a new anti-Christian campaign broke out and Chen, two other seminarians, and a young Catholic woman were arrested and martyred by decapitation.

Chen became one of the most famous members of the Holy Childhood. He was beatified by Pope Pius X in 1909 and in 1920 his relics were transferred to Notre Dame in Paris.[13] On that occasion the apostolic vicar of Zhejiang Province, Paul-Marie Reynard, claimed that the number of Chinese children who had died after baptism had reached twenty-two million. He based this figure on the number of children's cemeteries that had been created in China, such as the cemetery of the Holy Childhood in Ningbo, where ten thousand children were said to be buried. In 2000 Chen was canonized by Pope John Paul II and included in a list of 120 martyrs of the Catholic Church in China; this list aroused tremendous controversy in mainland China. In addition, an altar at Notre Dame in Paris was dedicated to the Holy Childhood. It depicted Jesus joining the hand of a European child with the hand of a Chinese child. China remained the priority area of the Holy Childhood and one-third of its allocations were still being sent to the China missions as late as 1950, the last year before the new Chinese Communist government suspended foreign missions. The Holy Childhood's priority on aiding Chinese children saved it from being absorbed into Propaganda (Sacred Congregation for the Propagation of the Faith).[14]

The romanticized Catholic sensibility surrounding the Holy Childhood is depicted in the membership cards reproduced in figures 5.2 and 5.3. The cards were meant to be personalized with a name and date. Figure 5.2 bears a Dutch inscription and states that a P. L. M. Van Rompaey was enrolled as a member of the Society of the Holy Childhood (H. Kindsheid) on November 1, 1858. It depicts an imaginative scene in China of abandoned children being saved by missionaries and European children. One priest in the foreground has waded into the water to save drowning infants who have been thrown into the water by uncaring parents. The priest in the middle of the illustration appears to be administering baptism to abandoned infants who have been gathered by a Chinese associate and put into a basket. To the left, a nun is holding a child. There is no distinction in physical features between the European and the Chinese

Figure 5.2. A membership card in Dutch for the Society of the Holy Childhood (H. Kindsheid). The card contains a blank space that was filled in with a name (P. L. M. Van Rompaey) and a date (1 November 1858). The priest in the foreground is saving Chinese children from being drowned in the stream while the priest at the center is baptizing abandoned Chinese infants from a basket in which they have been gathered by a Chinese associate. To the left, a Chinese nun holds an infant. Two distinctly European girls are present and assisting. In the case on the left, the girl is pushing a pig away to prevent it from eating the child. Provenance: KADOC (formerly Katholiek Documentatie Centrum), Katholieke Universiteit Leuven, Belgium.

Nº 1. L

Accipe puerum istum et nutri mihi:
ego dabo tibi mercedem tuam. *(Ex Ch 2 V 9)*

Societati Sanctæ Infantiæ nomen dedit

_____ *die* _____

Figure 5.3. A membership card in Latin for the Society of the Holy Childhood (Societas Sanctae Infantiae) ca. 1850. The space for a name and date are blank. The life-threatening danger to the Chinese infants of being eaten by the pig (left) and dog (right) is contrasted with the sweet, smiling faces of the European children who save them from this horrible fate. This portrayal de-emphasizes the worldly and transient reality that most of these abandoned infants were moribund and would survive only long enough to be baptized. At the same time, the drawing emphasizes the spiritual reality by portraying two children swimming at the top to represent the happier fate of eternal salvation in paradise for these baptized children. The priest wears an Episcopal cross and bears a resemblance to Mgr. Forbin-Janson, the founder of the Holy Childhood. Provenance: KADOC (formerly Katholiek Documentatie Centrum), Katholieke Universiteit Leuven, Belgium.

children, although the man holding the basket is distinguished by Chinese facial features and a darker complexion. So while the adults reflect racial differences, the children do not.

Two small girls representing the Holy Childhood are assisting the priests and nun. One is pushing a pig away from a child on the ground, presumably saving the child from being eaten by the pig. Of course, there were practically no European children in China at that time and the picture was not meant to be taken literally. The card embodied a childlike religiosity that de-emphasized any sign that many of these abandoned children were moribund and would die shortly after being baptized. The picture was meant to appeal to a child's imagination in a way that often appears in children's literature and conveys a different meaning from the more literal reality of adults. European children would be present in China through the force of their prayers and penny contributions. Their spiritual purity would constitute a force that would help to save Chinese children not only from the horrors of marauding pigs and dogs but also from their parents' abandonment, exposure to the wet and cold, and eternal damnation.

Figure 5.3 is a blank membership card of the Holy Childhood, inscribed in Latin. The inscription below the picture is a quotation from Exodus 2:9 in which Pharaoh's daughter, having discovered the infant Moses floating in the water, said to the Hebrew woman (actually Moses's mother): "Take this child away, and nurse him for me, and I will give you wages" (RSV). Sometimes abandoned Chinese children were also placed on small rafts in the water, so the spiritual parallel between God saving Moses and the Chinese children would have been clearly in mind to those seeing this devotional card. This card depicts a priest holding a Chinese child as he is surrounded by three European girls who are protecting the Chinese children from being eaten by a dog (on the lower right) and a pig (on the lower left). The dog appears to be snarling, but there is no fear in the children's faces because their purity, as blessed by God, enables them to triumph over evil and adversity. The children at the top of the picture are apparently Chinese children who, washed in the water of baptism, have gone to heaven. The priest wears an episcopal cross and bears a resemblance to a portrait of Forbin-Janson, the founder of the Holy Childhood.

For those of us looking at this card today, these angelic, smiling faces of children are jarring because they seem to contradict the dire reality of the fate facing these abandoned Chinese infants. But, as with the previous devotional card, the card was meant to be read with a child's imagination. The horrors of adult reality were de-emphasized while childlike hope, innocence, and purity were stressed. The purity of the children's prayers and penny contributions would enable the missionaries to save the abandoned Chinese children from voracious pigs and dogs. They would be fed and clothed and housed in orphanages built with the Holy Childhood contributions. And they would be baptized into eternal salvation. This was the vision of China that many late-nineteenth-century European children absorbed in a way that left a long-lasting image in their minds.

It was well known in the nineteenth century that the Jesuit missionaries to China, from their arrival in 1582 until the order's temporary dissolution in 1773, had been the most knowledgeable observers of China. Although the Jesuits' ambition and arrogance evoked harsh criticism from other Europeans, their scholarly training enabled them to understand Chinese culture and society in ways that non-Jesuit missionaries trained primarily in evangelism could not. Sarcey certainly knew this because many of the most eminent eighteenth-century China Jesuits were French. And yet among the sources on China that he cited in his series of articles on the "Little Chinese," there are no Jesuit authors. This was apparently because the Jesuit accounts of infanticide contradicted his argument.

In place of Jesuit sources, Sarcey cited two non-Jesuit missionaries to China. One of them was the Spanish Augustinian Juan Mendoza, whose history of China published in Rome in 1585 became famous because of its pioneering observations rather than its depth or comprehensiveness.[15] In any case, Mendoza did not deny the existence of infanticide, but simply had not observed it during his brief and limited stay in China. Sarcey's other main missionary source was the French Lazarist Évarist-Régis Huc (1813–1860).[16] Huc was based in Mongolia starting in 1841 and made a long journey across the northern border regions of China to Tibet in 1844–1846. His famous account of this journey appeared in seven editions between 1850 and 1868 and was translated into several foreign languages.[17] The book received such an enthusiastic reception that, after returning to France in 1852, he tried to follow it up with a sequel but without success.[18]

Sarcey's use of Huc's book to make his argument against the Jesuits shows how polemics obscured the facts of the debate over infanticide. Although Huc's book was widely regarded as more entertaining than factual in nature, it was—apart from some inaccurate details and dates—a reliable source.[19] But while Huc's book was accurate, his position on infanticide in China was not as clear-cut as Sarcey maintained. Although Huc rarely mentioned the fact, he had not made his famous journey from Mongolia to Tibet alone, but had been accompanied by his religious superior, Joseph Gabet (1808–1853). And Gabet gathered the very clear impression that infanticide was widespread in China.[20] In fact, after this journey, Gabet returned to Paris to write a short book entitled *Un mot sur l'infanticide en Chine* (A word on infanticide in China), in which he argued that female infanticide in China was very extensive.

Gabet also had an agenda. The priority that writing this little book received from Gabet upon his return to Europe (it was dated February 9, 1847) indicates that it was linked to the urgent effort to promote the fundraising of the Holy Childhood and was an attempt to rebut the infanticide deniers in Europe who were impeding that effort. In the preface, Gabet spoke about an attempt to "disperse certain prejudices against the work of the Holy Childhood which claimed that there were a large number of victims of infanticide in the Chinese empire."[21] He made numerous laudatory references to the Holy Childhood, which he noted was founded in Paris only four years before by Forbin-Janson.

Gabet gave no indication of having any disagreement with Huc and, in fact, cited from one of Huc's books several times. The fact is that Huc's statements on infanticide were too mixed to lend themselves easily to polemics. He noted, on one hand, that female infanticide was extensively practiced in China. On the other hand, he criticized certain missionaries for writing exaggerated accounts that implied that the Chinese government and public opinion tolerated the practice.[22] Huc obscured his position even further when in a later work he appeared to contradict his earlier reservations by writing that "it is incontestable that infanticides are very numerous in China."[23] Unfortunately, in this polemical battle involving infanticide, the subtleties of the arguments were overwhelmed by the vehemence of the debate.

It is not known exactly when Sarcey's series of articles on the Little Chinese came to the attention of the Jesuits in Shanghai. With the opening of the Suez Canal in 1869, the distance between Europe and China was halved and steamship passage was reduced to two months. Copies of *Le XIXe Siècle* with Sarcey's articles probably arrived in Shanghai in February 1876. Given this paper's hostility to the Jesuits, copies of it would have made for prompt reading and lively discussion in the reading room at the Jesuit complex of Zikawei. One of those Jesuits who was most outraged by Sarcey's articles was Palatre.

CREATING A FOREIGN ISLAND IN CHINA

Prior to 1800 the Jesuits in China had been the most important cultural intermediaries between China and Europe. They wrote the most informative books about China in Europe and they made the most effective presentation of Europe and Christianity to the Chinese. After the Society of Jesus was reconstituted in 1814, they returned to China; however, times had changed and when the Jesuits returned to China in 1841 they had an experience that was very different from their earlier one. The old Jesuits had encountered a sophisticated culture that placed the bar of entry very high for foreign religious teachings. A remarkably capable group of Jesuits had met that challenge and established a fledgling Christian church in China. After Matteo Ricci established a Jesuit base in Beijing in 1601, the Jesuits devoted much of the next two centuries to working through the imperial court. However, this program failed to establish Christianity as a lasting force in the capital. While the old Jesuits had served as imperial advisers and tutors in the seventeenth century, by the eighteenth century they were increasingly reduced to craftsman status, painting imperial portraits or serving as technicians in the Astronomical Bureau.

The new Jesuits returning to China arrived in the wake of Great Britain's military defeats of the Chinese in the Opium War (1839–1842).[24] They bypassed Beijing and established their headquarters in Shanghai. The contrast between the old imperial capital and the new commercial and colonialist center reflected the shifting realities of power. With the imperial court no longer the intermediary, there was a much more direct interaction between European missionaries and Chinese Christians. The conflicts that occurred were far less about international political relations between Rome and Beijing and far more about local religious authority.

The new Jesuits had a different mentality from the old Jesuits. Whereas the old Jesuits had to build the church from nothing, the new Jesuits encountered a Chinese church that was already becoming Sinicized by Chinese priests and catechists. While the earlier Rites Controversy had involved a mixture of theological and cultural issues, the conflicts between the new Jesuits and the Chinese Christians involved questions of power more than theology. In spite of the imperialist attitudes that blighted their return to China, the Jesuits' scholarly traditions soon reasserted themselves and the Jesuits became, once again, important cultural intermediaries between China and Europe. While the Protestant missionaries excelled at establishing schools and universities in China, they never surpassed the scholarly output of the Jesuits. As notable examples, the Jesuits were responsible for assembling two priceless literary treasures for China: the old Jesuits created the Beitang Library in Beijing, and the new Jesuits created the Zikawei Library in Shanghai.[25]

The Jesuit base at Zikawei was established in 1847 when the Jesuit superior, Fr. Claude Gotteland, directed Father Lemaître to purchase property four miles outside of the city of Shanghai adjacent to the burial site of the eminent scholar-official and convert Xu Guangqi (1562–1633) (see map 3).[26] One branch of Xu's family had remained faithful Catholics over the years and had built a small chapel on this family property at a site called Zi-ka-wei (Xujiahui, literally, "Xu family village"). Lamaître purchased a piece of land adjoining this chapel and here the first Jesuit residence was built and occupied in July 1848. The Jesuits established their headquarters at Zikawei and proceeded to build an impressive missionary complex there.

The Lower Yangzi River region had long been the center of commerce, wealth, and culture in China. It was called Jiangnan (literally, "the southern part of the Yangzi River"), initially the name of a province in the Ming dynasty but later subdivided by the Qing rulers into Jiangsu and Anhui provinces. During the Ming and Qing periods, its commercial centers were at the old cities of Nanjing and Wuxi. But after 1842, the vibrant city of Shanghai, located at the eastern edge of Jiangnan, began to emerge as a hybrid of Chinese enterprise and Western colonialism. It was divided into several foreign trading spheres and an older Chinese City where the Chinese officials had their offices. The most important of these spheres was the British Settlement (later called the International Settlement). The American Settlement lay to the north, beyond the Suzhou Creek, and to the south lay the French Settlement.

Unlike Hong Kong with its majestic views from steep hills that rise out of the sea, the area around Shanghai sits on the eastern side of a flat alluvial plain, then broken only by numerous canals and large lakes.[27] The nearest low hills lay thirty-five miles to the southwest, near Songjiang. Shanghai soil was low and marshy, and any digging struck water five or ten feet below the surface. This made the construction of buildings more expensive because they required pilings. Bricks were used extensively in construction. The temperatures in Shanghai ranged from a wintry low of twenty-five degrees Fahrenheit to a summertime high of ninety-six degrees, with sudden twenty-degree temperature swings being common in the spring and autumn. Shanghai experienced very warm, humid summers and temperate winters, although snow usually fell in December and January. European residents needed their thickest clothing and furs in the winter and the thinnest fabrics in the summer. The annual rainfall was fifty inches, with constant rain and dampness from January to April.

Northern Europeans were not well suited to the climate and food supply of Shanghai. Most suffered chronic diarrhea due to the impure water and liquid manure used in agriculture. Europeans were slow to adopt healthful Chinese habits, such as tea drinking. Because diarrhea, dysentery, and cholera were traced to the eating of Chinese fruits and vegetables, Europeans tended to have a diet of meats (beef, mutton, chicken, bacon, and ham), rich dairy products (pudding, pastry, jelly, custard, blancmange, cheese, and butter), and alcoholic beverages (sherry, Champagne, beer, port, claret, Moselle, and Burgundy). The only Chinese vegetable considered safe to eat was rice. Europeans believed that a residence in Shanghai reduced one's strength and energy and increased vulnerability to illness. For this reason, frequent trips to other localities (Japan, the

Yangzi River, the northern ports and Ningbo) were considered essential for preserving one's health.

There was a good road linking Shanghai and Zikawei. It had been built in the 1850s by the British Royal Engineers and funded by the Chinese government in order to defend against the Taiping rebels.[28] The road was well maintained by public subscription and provided a means for pedestrian traffic, riding, and carriage drives. A favorite evening amusement in Shanghai involved taking a carriage drive west on Nanjing Road past the Racecourse to the Bubbling Well, at which point the road branched off to the north and the south. Taking the branch three miles to the south brought one to Zikawei. The road passed through fields cultivated almost entirely with cotton, which provided yellow flowers in the spring and white cotton bolls in the fall. The stark flatness of the cotton fields was interrupted only by villages with peach and pear orchards and grave mounds in cemeteries surrounded by cedar trees.

Although the Jesuits at Zikawei shared many customs with the Europeans at Shanghai, a European style of living would have been costly, and it is likely that the open country separating Shanghai from the Catholic complex brought the Jesuits a more blended way of life with a greater mixture of Chinese and European customs. This blending would have been fostered by the increasing number of Chinese seminarians, nuns, and orphans who populated Zikawei.

Extensive flooding throughout Jiangnan in 1849 followed by famine in 1850 produced many abandoned children. The Jesuits gathered some of these children in separate orphanages for boys and girls, initially at Caijiawan (Tsai-kia-ouan), near Huangtang, in 1849.[29] The orphanages had to be dispersed in 1861 because of attacks by the Taiping rebels. In 1864 they were reestablished at Zikawei, four miles away. The site was called Touse-wei (Tushanwan), which means "hillock at the bend of the canal."[30] As part of the vocational training program at the Tou-sé-wei orphanage, a printing press was established there and by 1869 the boys had already cut the printing blocks for over seventy religious books written by the old Jesuits.[31] The program began with wood-block printing and added metal type by 1874, eventually producing a long list of scholarly monographs in the Variétés Sinologiques series.

The first European-style Chinese community of Catholic sisters was established at Zikawei in 1855 when the motherhouse of the Sisterhood of the Presentation was founded.[32] It became the largest women's order in China. Drawing most of its members from the lower classes, the Presentadines sent their sisters into the interior of China to work with women and children.[33] In 1872 the Jesuits established a center for research at Zikawei that eventually included a museum of natural history and a meteorological, astronomical, and magnetic observatory that issued daily weather reports and forecasts.[34] Later a library and a secondary school (St. Ignatius School) were joined by Aurora University in 1908, although the university was later moved from Zikawei to another site in the French Concession. The four-and-a-half-acre Zikawei site was capped by the large St. Ignatius Cathedral with its two prominent spires.

The Zikawei Library was initially housed in three rooms of the first Jesuit residence occupied in 1848.[35] The increase in acquisitions forced the library to move to a larger facility in 1860. A more permanent twelve-room, two-story stone building was completed in 1906. After the Communist Liberation, the local government of Shanghai closed the library and confiscated the contents in 1953. Some of the material was moved to the public library of Shanghai, where it was protected from the destructive rampages of the Red Guards during the Cultural Revolution. Late in the twentieth century when subway construction threatened the library building's structure, the rest of the books were moved to storage. The Zikawei Library was reopened as a branch of the Shanghai Library in 2003.

THE JESUIT RESPONSE TO INFANTICIDE DENIERS

In an age of world trade when copyright and intellectual property rights preoccupy us, the Jesuit tradition of collaborative authorship seems alien. Yet the fact is that the name appearing on a book produced by the Jesuits often was only the last in a series of authors whose individual contributions frequently went unmentioned. This situation was due to the Jesuits' religious vows, their scholarly nature, and projects that required many years to complete.[36] A project might require the expertise of more than one scholar. Frequently, authors would fall ill and die while the project was in progress, requiring others to finish it. Finally, the sense of personal ownership common among authors was diminished by the Jesuit spirit of teamwork and common goal reflected in their Latin motto, *Ad majorem Dei gloriam* ("For the greater glory of God"), often abbreviated to A.M.D.G., which appeared as a dedicatory formula in their books. The title page of Palatre's *L'infanticide et l'oeuvre de la Sainte-Enfance en Chine* (Infanticide and the work of the Holy Childhood in China) contains the abbreviation A.M.D.G., signifying the spirit of Jesuit collaboration involved in this book.

In a religious society of outstanding men, Gabriel Palatre was not particularly exceptional. He stands out for only one reason: His name appears on this scholarly and thorough response to Sarcey's charges. It is a passionate response, but the passion and polemics belong to an old and largely forgotten controversy. Eventually most people lost interest in this debate over infanticide in China, causing the book *L'infanticide* to lie buried, practically untouched in libraries and rarely studied for over a century. Denial and silence descended on this depressing topic. For us today, *L'infanticide* is of interest for reasons that Palatre would have considered secondary.

Palatre was born at Châteaugiron (diocese of Rennes) in France on July 2, 1830. He became a novice in the Jesuit order in September 1853 at twenty-three years of age. After ten years of study and preparation, he departed for the Jiangnan mission in 1863. As is typical of Jesuits, he took his final vows relatively late—1866, when he was thirty-six years old. He apparently was frail: His evangelical activity in the districts surrounding Zikawei and in directing the boys' orphanage of Tou-sé-wei at the Zikawei complex did not last long.[37] After five years, infirmities forced him to reduce his physical activities. He became secretary to the monsignor vicar apostolic and scribe of the mission. His last years in the mission were consumed with writing his response to Sarcey's charges.

Palatre needed a collaborator to translate the Chinese texts that formed such an important part of his rebuttal to Sarcey. He found this collaborator in the Jesuit Olivier Durandière, who was twelve years his junior. Born in France in 1842, Durandière entered the Jesuit order in 1866, the year Palatre took his final vows. He went to China in 1868 and was assigned to Huaian, in northern Jiangsu Province. He was consecrated as a priest in 1872. Historical records describe Durandière as a mild and self-effacing man with a childlike obedience—zealous and very charitable.[38] He remained in China for thirty-four years, dying there in 1902. Huaian had long been a Christian center, but by the late nineteenth century, its two hundred souls had become uninspired Christians. Perhaps Durandière was partly to blame for the uninspired state of the church there; perhaps he was more of an intellectual than an evangelist. He coped with the boredom of his twelve years there by studying Chinese and translating sixty-six Chinese documents for Palatre. These documents form the main body of evidence for the book *L'infanticide*.

L'infanticide consists of approximately eighty-six thousand words divided into three parts. The first part (pages 1–114) lists proofs for the frequency of infanticide in China. These include official proclamations (chapter 1), moralistic stories (*shanshu*) colored by popular Buddhism and Daoism (chapter 2), Confucian essays against infanticide (chapter 3), newspaper articles (chapter 4), and popular images of infanticide (chapter 5). The second part of the book (pages 115–82) deals with Christian charity to alleviate infanticide. These include the baptism of moribund infants (chapter 6), feeding infants (chapter 7), and establishing orphanages (chapter 8). The third part deals with Chinese philanthropic efforts to deal with infanticide (pages 183–203). These include the failure of the Chinese to implement their plans of establishing orphanages (chapter 9), and the causes of infanticide (chapter 10). The sixty-six Chinese documents follow in a seventy-four-page appendix of documentary evidence. There are six folded leaves of illustrations.

The Chinese sources that the Jesuits used in compiling their work on infanticide included some of the most important works of popular morality then being published. Ten of the sixty-five documents were drawn from *Deyi lu* (Record of useful things). This was a comprehensive collection on performing charitable deeds with an emphasis on teaching morality, and it had a great influence in the late Qing and early Republic periods. The work was compiled by Yu Zhi of Wuxi in Jiangsu Province.[39] It was published in Suzhou in eight sections in 1869 and reprinted many times. A sixteen-section edition appeared in 1885. The Jesuits made extensive use of the chapter dealing with female infanticide titled "Regulations of the Infant Protection Societies."[40]

On March 1, 1877, Palatre sent a copy of the manuscript to the Holy Childhood office in Paris, but the director, Father de Giardin, delayed publishing it because of the cost of printing and other difficulties.[41] In frustration, and with a sense of his own mortality shadowing him due to his deterioriating health, Palatre undertook to produce an autograph copy of his own text for publication. A lithographic reproduction of the manuscript was published in a print run of only two hundred copies. Lithography involves a process of printing from a flat stone or metal plate. A page of manuscript written in ink is placed on this surface spread with a greasy material, followed by water and ink. The greasy parts repel the water but absorb the ink, creating a flat print plate that can be used in printing paper. This autograph edition was printed at Zikawei by the Tou-sé-wei orphanage press in 1878, three years after Sarcey's articles appeared.

The handwriting composing the text tells an additional story almost as touching as the infanticides it describes. Palatre probably sensed that he was running out of time, so completing this manuscript became his glorious obsession. Either his declining health or his stroke caused him to stop copying the manuscript for publication halfway through the book. He died on August 11, 1878, twenty-five years after becoming a Jesuit and sixteen years after arriving in the Jiangnan mission.

The style of handwriting changes at the break between pages 109 and 110, indicating that someone else took over and finished the project. The other author was probably a Jesuit confrere at Zikawei. Given that the book had already been a collaborative effort between Palatre and Durandière, the concluding work would have merely continued the collaboration in a typical Jesuit manner. Palatre apparently wrote the preface first—he dated it December 21, 1876. However, the foreword (*avertissement*) was written last and in a different style of handwriting: It refers to the "more than three years" (1876–1878) that elapsed between Sarcey's articles and the appearance of the book *L'infanticide* in Europe. By that point Palatre was probably already dead.

Exactly who might have taken over finishing the manuscript is a mystery, but it is possible to identify two other collaborators who contributed to the book. Palatre's use of Chinese romanizations is consistent and fairly knowledgeable, which would indicate that he had some knowledge of Chinese. However, the Chinese characters inserted into the main text, mostly in the footnotes, were written with a native facility that points to an unnamed Chinese collaborator. Possibly Palatre left blanks in his French text that a native Chinese calligraphist filled in with a Chinese brush, which clearly contrasts with Palatre's ink pen. The Chinese calligraphy of the sixty-six documents in the appendix appears to have been written by the same person. Palatre would have had no difficulty in finding a Chinese calligraphist among the Chinese at Zikawei.

A fourth collaborator was the French Jesuit Louis (Aloysius) Pfister (Fei Laizhi) (1833–1891). Pfister was three years younger than Palatre and had arrived at Zikawei in 1867, four years after Palatre. Pfister was in charge of the Zikawei Library and was engaged in compiling a detailed catalog of Jesuits who had worked in China from the founding of the mission by St. Francis Xavier in 1552 until the suppression of the Society of Jesus in 1773. He was a scholar as well as a librarian and certainly would have worked closely with Palatre in locating the many mission-related books that Palatre cited from in *L'infanticide*.

It is possible that Pfister established a pattern of collaboration that was repeated at the end of his own life. When Pfister died in 1891, his catalog of Jesuits who participated in the China mission was not in publishable form. A group of Jesuits led by Fr. Henri Bernard (Pei Huaxing) corrected errors, filled in lacunae, added Chinese characters, and compiled an index.[42] However, when Pfister's catalog was finally published in 1932–1934, Bernard's name appeared nowhere to take credit. Possibly Bernard was repeating the same editorial service that Pfister had performed in 1878 for Palatre and perhaps that is why Pfister's name appears nowhere in *L'infanticide*.[43]

There was a tension between Christianity and Chinese religious teachings over combating female infanticide. The Jesuits gathered a collection of Chinese documents that presented a remarkably clear picture of Chinese attempts to combat the practice. Confucianism, Buddhism, and Daoism all opposed infanticide although there were ambiguities in both Confucianism and Daoism. While the Jesuits were critical of the Chinese for being ineffectual in stopping the practice, it is likely that infanticide was so entrenched in China, particularly in rural areas, that it would have been exceedingly difficult to end.

Palatre believed that Christianity could provide a moral transformation of Chinese culture that would end infanticide, but eradicating infanticide was not simply a matter of moral transformation. Nor was it merely an economic matter of dealing with poverty. Female infanticide was rooted very deeply in Chinese culture. Palatre did not understand Chinese culture sufficiently to grasp this but, ironically, he was the intermediary of Chinese documents that do give us a glimpse into the cultural depth of this custom. Palatre summarized the tension between Christian and Chinese teachings near the end of part 1 of the book: "We have described the evil [of infanticide] in all its ugliness. Two powers are at work to bring a remedy: Catholicism and paganism, and it remains for us to demonstrate which side is meeting with success."[44]

6

✝

Christian Mission
Efforts to Aid Foundlings

SEVENTEENTH-CENTURY
EFFORTS TO SAVE EXPOSED CHILDREN

Prior to the nineteenth century, China missionaries spoke mainly of saving abandoned children in the spiritual sense. All Catholics were obliged to assist in this process, even to the point of secretly baptizing a child without the parents' permission. Their obligations were described in a list of forty-five regulations of the church composed in Chinese by the Jesuit Feliciano Pacheco (Cheng Jili) around 1670 in Canton. Article 19 addressed the matter of abandoned infants as follows:

> The rules and the formulas for valid administration of baptism in urgent cases should be learned by all [Christians], both men and women. If a non-Christian family takes an aversion to having a large number of children and seeks to kill a newborn, the Christians, knowing it, should do everything possible to save it and, if they cannot save its body, they should at least save its soul. If the parents do not allow it, it is necessary to baptize the child secretly, and be careful not to stand by idly and indifferent to its fate.
> The Christian women should also be on their guard for the case of a difficult childbirth. As soon as the child is born, they should quickly secure its salvation by baptizing it. If Christian childhood physicians treat the illness of the child and are unable to rescue it, at least they have attended to saving its soul and will thus one day have great merit before God.[1]

The most notable of the early missionary efforts to help abandoned children in China was led by Fr. Alfonso Vagnone (1568–1640). From 1605 until 1617, he led the mission at Nanjing, but the persecution of Shen Que led to Vagnone's expulsion to Canton. He changed his Chinese name from Wang Fengsu to Gao Yizhi and reentered China in 1624. He went to Shanxi Province, where he established a mission at Jiangzhou. During the 1634 great famine there, Vagnone was touched by the widespread abandonment of children. Using the mission subsidy sent from Macau, Vagnone bought a house and opened a foundling hospice.[2] On the first day he gathered fifty abandoned children, but his resources were soon overwhelmed by the task. He was assisted in his efforts by literati converts in Jiangzhou, including Duan Gun (baptized as Peter) and Han Lin and their families.[3] Duan Gun (Palatre refers to him as Pierre Tong) was particularly notable in his devotion to abandoned children. He was the president of a Congregation of Holy Angels (*Tianshenhui*) consisting of forty literati. Duan transformed his house into a public hospice into which he took one hundred abandoned children. When poor people came to his home, he gave them rice.

Duan shocked people by going into the street to gather abandoned children. By personally gathering these children, he was transgressing the sharp division in Chinese society between those who worked with their minds and those who worked with their hands. When his wife claimed that this sort of work should be done by servants and workers, he smiled and ignored her. But gradually, his family was won over and one of his sisters offered her jewels to Vagnone to pay the costs of maintaining his hospice. One day at a site just outside the city wall, Duan heard the cries of a child recently buried in a shallow grave. He dug it up and took it home, where his servants refused to wash it because of the filth and stench of its body. Duan washed the child himself and took care of it. He became a notable model of Christian charity in Jiangzhou.

After the Manchus conquered Ming China in 1644 and established the Qing dynasty, they asked the Jesuit Adam Schall to continue in the Bureau of Astronomy, and they gave him a plot of valuable land in the heart of Beijing upon which he built the Nantang (South Church). Following the example of the church in Nanjing, the Christians in Beijing were divided into six congregations (three for men and three for women) that met five times each month. Although each congregation differed in its membership, all were obliged to baptize abandoned children in the streets.[4]

In the south of China, the Dominican father Vitorio Ricci attempted to minister to both the spiritual and physical needs of abandoned children. Ricci is best known for his service to the Southern Ming loyalist warlord Zheng Chenggong (Koxinga), who drove the Dutch from Taiwan in 1661.[5] In 1656 on the island of Amoy off the Fujian coast, Ricci collected the youngest of the abandoned children and fed them. After exhausting his resources, he went from house to house begging for food for the older children. He wrote to the Dominican superior in Manila, asking for help in feeding these abandoned children.[6] He described these pathetic children, some still breast-feeding, others aged two, three, and four, who were covered with scabies and vermin and constantly crying. Famished and too busy to break from washing and dressing them, he ate their baby cereal and sugar mixture. But their numbers were increasing and the situation was so desperate that he said if alms were not forthcoming, he would die with the children.

Later when an epidemic struck Amoy in 1657, the population was decimated. Ricci passed himself off as a physician, and together with Father Zen of the indigenous clergy, he visited moribund children in their homes and baptized them. Although the parents were present and did not object, they were not Christians and had no understanding of the meaning of baptism.[7]

In Canton and nearby Foshan in the years 1659–1664, the Italian Jesuit Giovanni Lubelli devoted himself to helping exposed children. Not only did he minister to them spiritually by baptizing more than four hundred such children, but he also dealt with their material needs.[8] He helped to find them wet nurses and he placed those who survived with Christian families who would raise them.

Candida Xu (1607–1680) established one of the first Christian foundling hospices, in the second half of the seventeenth century in Songjiang in southern Jiangsu Province.[9] She was a granddaughter of the eminent scholar-official and convert Xu Guangqi, who had been baptized in 1604. The Xu family became devout patrons of the Catholic Church, and their family land at Xujiahui (Zikawei) provided the Jesuits with their most notable base of operations in China. Xu became famous in Europe for her piety and patronage of the church when the Jesuit missionary Philippe Couplet published a biography of her in Paris in 1688.[10] After marrying a wealthy and powerful man whom she converted to Christianity, she was widowed at the age of thirty. Perpetuating her grandfather's zeal and piety, she distributed alms, built churches and chapels, embroidered the draperies for the church altars, served as a catechist to her family, established sodalities, and supported catechists propagating the Gospel. Finally, she gathered a group of women together and taught them the baptism formula to be used on children in danger of dying when they assisted non-Christian women in childbirth.[11]

Wanting to go beyond baptizing moribund infants and procuring wet nurses for their survival, Xu sought out the assistance of her son Xu Zuanzeng (baptized Basil), who was an eminent scholar and official. He secured permission from the viceroy of Suzhou for her to buy a large house to found an orphanage. The governor and other officials contributed and, with her son's support, she was able to implement her plan in 1675. [12] Many of the children were so ill that more than two hundred died each year. She purchased land for a cemetery and personally furnished the coffins and shrouds for their burials. This orphange in Songjiang did not last long and appears to have closed when Madame Xu died in 1680.

EIGHTEENTH-CENTURY CHRISTIAN FOUNDLING HOSPICES

Catholic efforts to establish foundling hospices were frustrated in the eighteenth century by the lack of funds. In 1700 Fr. Joseph Prémare wrote a letter from Jiangxi Province to Fr. Charles Le Gobien, the Jesuit procurator at Paris, expressing the wish of several China missionaries that Christian foundling hospices be established in five or six of the largest provincial capitals.[13] These hospices for exposed children would house mostly girls and be run by pious women. Not until shortly before the French Revolution in 1789 were the missionaries able to establish a foundling hospice in Beijing, but the lack of mission funds hindered the establishment of others elsewhere.[14]

In a tone strange (if not morbid) to modern ears, the Jesuit father Jean-François Foucquet wrote in 1702 that the baptism of moribund children was preferable to baptizing adults. While converted adults might lose interest and fall away from the faith, thus endangering their salvation, abandoned children died immediately after baptism and came infallibly to heaven.[15] When Father François Noël returned to Europe as Jesuit procurator in 1703, he addressed a report to the Jesuit father-general in Rome in which he spoke of missed opportunities for baptism. He wrote that due to the lack of catechists, each year in Beijing alone, out of thirty thousand small children exposed in the streets, only three thousand were baptized.[16] If the Jesuits could increase the number of catechists to between twenty and thirty, all of these exposed children could be baptized. This could be achieved by affluent prelates in Rome or laypersons in other European cities contributing fifty or sixty guldens (a gold coin of the Netherlands and Germany) per year to support each catechist.

The baptizing of moribund children even reached into the Manchu imperial family. Sunu (Sourinama) (ca. 1648–1725) was the great-great-grandson of the Qing dynastic patriarch Nurhaci and a fourth cousin of the Yongzheng emperor (r. 1723–1735).[17] Sunu served the Kangxi emperor in the latter's military campaigns and was rewarded with high honors and position, including being raised to a prince of the fourth degree. However, in the struggle over the Kangxi emperor's successor, Sunu and his sons backed a losing candidate and in 1724 were exiled to Shanxi Province by the successful candidate, the Yongzheng emperor. It is unknown whether Sunu was ever baptized, but several of his sons were. The first to be baptized was Shu'erchen, who in 1719 was baptized as Paul by the Jesuit father José Soares (Suarez).[18] Paul was a devout and enthusiastic Christian who visited members of the royal family with mortally ill children and baptized the children by pouring water over their heads.[19]

In 1705 two Jesuit brothers skilled in medicine and pharmacy, Pierre Frapperie and Bernard Rodes, baptized a deathly ill little son of the third concubine of the Kangxi emperor and a moribund little daughter of a Manchu nobleman.[20] Palatre commented that "both were flown to heaven not on the back of the official dragon that legend is taken to serve the sovereign of China, but carried by the hands of angels who are better acquainted with the path to paradise."

This comment pitting the imperial dragon against Christian angels is revealing of Palatre and other nineteenth-century Jesuits in China. The earlier Jesuits who converted the members of the imperial family were isolated missionaries who had been forced to live on Chinese terms and to accommodate themselves to Chinese culture and the Manchu court. Nevertheless, they initiated the process of assimilating Christianity into Chinese culture. However, the nineteenth-century Jesuits were in a position of such colonialist strength that they were able to ignore the Manchu court at Beijing and build an island of European Christianity in Shanghai at Zikawei that viewed the surrounding sea of Chinese culture in hostile terms. Unaccommodating comments like Palatre's about angels displacing the Chinese dragon foreshadowed the coming storm of the following century that climaxed in 1966 when the Red Guards attacked Zikawei and dismantled the twin steeples of the St. Ignatius Cathedral.

Although there was a great deal of distrust of both the old (1540–1773) and new (post-1814) Jesuits in Europe, their critics often unwittingly confirmed how accurate the Jesuits were. One such critic was Fr. Matteo Ripa (1682–1746) of Naples, who went to China as a Propaganda missionary. Ripa served at the court of the Kangxi emperor as an artist from 1711 until 1723. After returning to Naples, he began in 1743 composing his memoirs, which were published posthumously. They are filled with lively details and were translated into English in an abridged and widely read edition that appeared in 1844. His vivid comments on female infanticide in China are included in both editions.

On February 22, 1711, while passing through an open field in central China en route to Beijing, Ripa found an abandoned girl (*projetta*) who was only a few days old.[21] She was moribund and although he baptized her with the name of Maria, dedicating her to the Virgin Mary and arranging for her care, she died soon thereafter. Ripa later learned that abandoned children were commonplace in China. He said that children were abandoned in China out of poverty, disability, and illegitimacy. Supposedly celibate Buddhist nuns abandoned them to hide their own sin of promiscuity. Ripa said that some of these children were thrown into a river and others were left along public roads in hopes that they might be adopted by passersby.

Ripa makes no mention of the fact that most of the exposed infants were girls, and his explanation of the causes of child abandonment is incomplete. Nor does he seem to have been aware that most infants were disposed of by being drowned in the privacy of their homes rather than being abandoned in public places. What makes his memoirs most valuable are his firsthand observations of the practice. In particular, he confirms the most shocking claim of the Chinese missionaries, namely, that some of the abandoned children were eaten by animals. Ripa himself claims to have seen one infant under the tusks of a swine and another between the teeth of a dog.[22] He says that the emperor provided for carts to go through the streets of Beijing each morning, gathering abandoned children. He claims they were taken to a Buddhist temple, where they were nursed by wet nurses, but that scarcely 10 percent of them survived.

One of the most detailed missionary sources on infanticide is found in the previously cited letter written in 1720 from Beijing by the French Jesuit François-Xavier Dentrecolles (1664–1741), describing a proposal for a foundling hospice.[23] The pre-1800 mission depended largely on the financial contributions of individual patrons, and the Jesuits were skilled in fund-raising techniques. One of these techniques involved compiling a list of benefactors and then having Jesuits in China write detailed letters that would inform them of activities in China, thank them for past support, and solicit them for further contributions. Dentrecolles wrote this letter to a wealthy lady in England of whom he knew nothing except that she had contributed liberally to the mission over several years. This lady's contributions had supported the catechists, whose main function was to go through the streets of Beijing each day, searching for abandoned infants to baptize. These baptisms involved a comprehensive effort and Dentrecolles claimed that the number of infants baptized each year in Beijing was usually over five or six thousand.

Not all of these baptized infants had been abandoned. In many cases, they were dying from smallpox or other illnesses, and the catechists arranged to accompany physicians on their house calls. Sometimes the baptisms were performed surreptitiously and without the parents' knowledge. Dentrecolles only briefly mentions that some of these infants were victims of female infanticide. Due to poverty, the family ordered the midwife to "bathe the infant" (suffocate the little girl in a basin of water). In order to secure the salvation of these girls, a female catechist would accompany the midwife to the delivery and secretly perform the baptism with holy water. A Buddhist temple (apparently the same temple mentioned by Ripa) in a densely populated section of Beijing gathered exposed children. For a small monthly sum, a catechist was allowed to enter the temple each day and administer baptism to moribund infants.

Several deathbed baptisms that Dentrecolles describes strike the modern reader as gruesome, but his sensibility belongs to a different age and there is little doubt that the concern for the salvation of these little girls' souls was genuine. Dentrecolles told of how a Christian in the imperial service was returning from work early one morning when he felt compelled to take an out-of-the-way path. (This fortuitous change in direction was viewed as a sign of divine guidance and it occurred in more than one missionary account of the baptism of a moribund child in China.[24]) Here he found an infant between the teeth of a pig that was about to devour it. He chased the pig and retrieved the bloody body of the infant, baptizing it before it expired.

Another Christian found an abandoned moribund child in a chest on the bank of a river and baptized it before it died. Yet another Christian very early one morning saw an empty chest outside the door of a house. Anticipating that it was there for the disposal of a newborn infant, he hid and waited. When the door opened and the moribund infant was placed in the chest, at the first chance he rushed forward with holy water and secretly baptized the child before it died. Yet another story involved a Christian physician sending a servant to a remote area to dig up a tree for transplanting. The servant came upon a hastily dug shallow grave and upon exploring found a little coffin which he opened to find a sickly child who was still breathing. The servant returned to inform his master, who took holy water and baptized the child, who died shortly thereafter.

Although the missionaries taught that the exposure of infants was immoral, the impact of their teaching was limited to church members. Any attempt to deal with the problem in a broader way through establishing foundling hospices involved costs that strained the funds at their disposal. There were also limits on their movements as foreigners who often lacked the native language fluency needed to gain access to moribund infants. Nevertheless, in spite of these obstacles, the eighteenth-century Catholic missionaries demonstrated profound concern about the plight of abandoned children.

In December 1720, the same year that Dentrecolles was writing his letter describing a Chinese ideal plan for a foundling hospice, the papal legate Mgr. Carlo Ambrogio Mezzabarba met with the Kangxi emperor.[25] While in China, Mezzabarba learned of the plight of abandoned children and, on his return to Rome, he pleaded their case to potential donors.[26] Due to his efforts, the procurator of Propaganda at Macau was able to devote four thousand écus (crowns) to feeding abandoned children. In 1735 the procurator requested a regular and permanent allocation for this purpose. The ministry extended throughout several provinces in China, but had its focus at Canton, where exposed children were collected in large numbers and were more easily raised.

The results were so positive that Propaganda attempted to create a fund that would assure the continuation of this ministry of charity. The pope, cardinals, and pious persons sent alms for the care of abandoned children in China. Propaganda ordered that a portion of these contributions be set aside to generate an annuity whose principal was placed in Manila. The Spanish procurator at Macau used these funds to gather poor children of Chinese gentiles whose parents had sold, exposed, or attempted to kill them. The children were sent to Manila to be raised in the Christian religion. This ministry lasted for ten years.

The Jesuit Maurice du Baudory devoted his ministry to abandoned children at Canton in the twenty years between his arrival in 1712 and his death in 1732. His newly arrived confrere Antoine Gaubil explained in a letter that there were two categories of abandoned children in Canton.[27] The first group was housed at government expense in the well-run House of Mercy foundling hospice (*yuying tang*). The other category of exposed children consisted of those carried to the Christian church, where they were immediately baptized and then fed. The plight of the second group was far more desperate than the first group because almost all of them were on the verge of death.

It was difficult to gain access to the government hospice. Consequently, the children there were not baptized until they were moribund. Because dealing with the officials in charge of the hospice was complicated and prickly, these officials were circumvented by secret arrangements with wet nurses and administrators who were paid an annual fee in exchange for access to the hospice. Since entry by a male missionary into a hospice filled with women would have violated Chinese propriety and inevitably come to the attention of the government officials, a female catechist was used. She was informed when a child was close to death, whereupon a wet nurse would bring the child to a designated area where the catechist would baptize it. The child would then be returned to its bed. The catechist would record the name of the baptized child and whether the child later died. The costs of maintaining this system included the salary of the catechist, gifts to the administrators and physicians, payments to the two staff members who informed the catechist about the sick children, and payments to the wet nurses who brought the child to be baptized. The total cost amounted to just over twenty taels of silver (or one hundred French francs) each year.

Missionaries kept careful records of the number of baptisms they performed. Du Baudory said that when they began in Canton in 1719 they baptized 136 abandoned children, and he expected the number to reach three hundred in 1722. These numbers were far smaller than those claimed for Beijing. The difference was probably due to the larger size of Beijing, the greater effort in terms of expenses and number of catechists in Beijing, and the tendency of certain Beijing fathers to exaggerate their numbers in order to create a more powerful impression in their reports to Europe.

The foundling hospices dealt primarily with infants and were not meant to serve as orphanages that housed older children. Children beyond infancy were placed in private homes for care. Du Baudory was concerned that baptism without Christian upbringing would be useless. Consequently, he and the catechist maintained an updated list of baptized children who had survived. Payments were made to the stewards of the hospice to place these baptized children with Christian families.

As for the abandoned children brought directly to the church, rather than to the government hospice, Du Baudory reported that the number of baptisms began with only five or six a year and rose in 1721 to forty-five children who died soon after baptism. As for the far smaller number who survived, he found a wet nurse for each one. The wet nurse was paid the equivalent of twenty-five sous per month. In Chinese currency, this amounted to approximately sixty-two copper cash.[28] In addition, he had to supply linens and medicines to cure ailments. At the beginning, it was difficult to find wet nurses, but it became much easier later. Du Baudory attempted to disengage himself as soon as possible from the process by placing these children in Christian families. In spite of his resources being extremely limited, he never refused to take a child, and when he wrote his letter in 1722, he was responsible for feeding eighteen children.

CATECHISTS AND CHRISTIAN VIRGINS

Catechists were a crucial part of the Christian ministry to abandoned children. In the urban areas, catechists played a secondary role to priests, and many were assigned to find abandoned children and baptize them. However, in the rural areas, catechists played a more important role as leaders. Largely because of governmental restrictions, the development of Catholicism in China began to diverge into rural and urban churches, a divergence that has become more pronounced over the years.[29] Because of the shortage of priests, many rural parishes in China never saw a priest for several years. Consequently, Catholics came to depend far more on the catechists and the heads of the local Christian communities than on priests.[30] They gave instruction, proselytized nonbelievers, distributed religious booklets and calendars, baptized children, and ministered to the sick and dying. They were the first to suffer during anti-Christian persecutions.

Some catechists were trained by individual missionaries and others were trained in a group, such as a confraternity of catechists. One of the first of these confraternities was established by the Jesuit Francesco Brancati in Jiangsu Province in 1664. It was called the Confraternity of Saint Francis Xavier (Sheng Fangjige Hui).[31] Catechetical instruction was a crucial component of pastoral work among Catholics in China.[32] The lack of knowledge of the fundamental teachings of Christianity, rather than persecution, was thought to have been the main reason for the falling away of Chinese Christians from the church. The lack of priests caused pastoral work to fall mainly to the catechists. Religious booklets were only a partial substitute for the lack of priests because many Chinese were illiterate. For this reason, neophytes were taught to memorize the catechism so that it would not be lost.[33] This practice melded well with Chinese culture, in which memorizing the Confucian classics had long been a standard part of Chinese education.

While there appears to have been some regional variations in the terms and responsibilities, catechists (*xianggong*) tended to function in similar ways throughout China. They were divided into those who traveled and those who had a fixed residence. Traveling, or itinerant, catechists (*chuanjiaoyuan* or *zou hui zhi ren*) were involved mainly in making converts. They were full-time employees who were paid for their living and traveling expenses. They often accompanied priests in the capacity of guides and assistants. Some of them were celibate because they performed the duties of priests.[34] There were both male itinerant catechists (*chuanjiao xiansheng*) and female itinerant catechists (*nü chuanjiao xiansheng*). The latter date from the seventeenth century and they played an important role in the church.

By contrast, residential catechists had fixed addresses and sometimes also were elders or congregational leaders (*huizhang*). They tended to be older, more literate, and married or widowed. They were responsible for discipline in their church, but they also consoled and supported Catholics in need. They were also responsible for the instruction of catechumens, whom they sometimes took into their homes during the period of instruction. They held prayer meetings and sometimes gave spiritual readings at the Sunday meetings. They also baptized infants and adults and conducted funeral services.

Because of the importance of catechists to the life of the church, the Catholic authorities enhanced the dignity of the catechists' office through installation ceremonies. In Sichuan Province, seminarians were required to serve as catechists for one year before advancing to the priesthood. In Jiangxi Province, the Chinese referred to catechists as *jiaotou* (religious headmen).[35] They played a crucial role in the conversion process through teacher-student relationships, and they also had the power to expel converts for misbehavior. Sometimes catechists were the main leaders of their congregations.

Because of the customary separation of the sexes in traditional Chinese society, it was difficult for male catechists and priests, particularly foreign priests, to establish contact with Chinese women. Consequently, Christian women filled this role. They worked as female catechists, giving religious instruction to other women and serving as baptizers (*quanxi xiansheng*).[36] European priests had trouble adapting to nineteenth-century Chinese society. European-style Catholic convents were not introduced to China until after the signing of the Sino-Western treaties, beginning with the Treaty of Nanjing (1842). When the Jesuits returned to China in 1841, they came with the attitude of conquerors. Their Eurocentrism caused them to clash with the indigenous Chinese church leadership that had developed in their absence. The Catholic clerics' patriarchal attitudes brought them into conflict with a uniquely Chinese organization known as the Christian Virgins, and the Chinese resisted their attempts to impose a hierarchical European church structure.[37]

The earliest religious communities for women in China were introduced in Fujian Province in the seventeenth century. The Jesuits had strictly observed the Chinese custom of separating the sexes in establishing separate chapels for women and in being very cautious in administering sacraments, particularly confirmation and confession, that involved close physical contact with women. However, the Dominicans in Fujian were less cautious. Not only did they arouse the criticism of local men by celebrating the sacraments with women, even at night and in secret, but they also encouraged women to take vows of chastity.[38] Female vows of chastity by unmarried virgins challenged the dominant Chinese practice of marriage for almost all women.

Borrowing the model of the *beata* (blessed women) that had been successful in the Philippines, the Spanish Dominicans introduced this form of quasi-religious community into China. Although unable to establish formal religious communities (*beaterios*), these Chinese women continued to live with their families, took private vows of chastity, and devoted themselves to the religious instruction of females in their household. Some women began using the institution of the *beatas* to acquire some degree of personal independence in their pursuit of religious devotion. Some transgressed Confucian modesty by visiting the friars at night for confession. Others threatened patriarchal dominance and the lineage structure by refusing to accept marriages that were arranged for them.

The next step in the development of women's religious communities in China involved the Christian Virgins. In the eighteenth century, the missionaries of the Missions Étrangères de Paris developed the Institute of Christian Virgins in the southwestern provinces of Sichuan, Yunnan, and

Guizhou.[39] These women lived at home and, at the age of twenty-five, they made vows of temporary chastity that could be renewed every three years. Many of them served as female catechists.

The Christian Virgins were one of the leading groups involved in the baptism of moribund children in nineteenth-century China. They were a uniquely Chinese institution and represented an important step in the adaptation of Christianity to Chinese culture. Unlike many of the forms of Catholic organizations in the hierarchy between the laity and clerics, such as confraternities, the Christian Virgins were less a duplication of a European model and more a spontaneous Chinese development. The group emerged out of the desire of certain Chinese women to devote themselves more fully to God's service. Although there was a tradition of celibate Buddhist and Daoist nuns, the preferred historical model for Christian Virgins was drawn from the Confucian ideal of a "chaste woman" (*zhennü*).[40] Most Christian Virgins were from affluent families, and their wealth enabled them to resist the traditional path of marriage. Resistance to marriage among Chinese women manifested itself in several ways in nineteenth-century China, and not all of it was associated with Christianity. In Sundak (Shunde) and other counties in the Canton delta, it gave rise to "never-to-be-married" sisterhoods.[41] These sworn spinsters (*zishu nü*) took formal vows of celibacy and continued to worship their natal family ancestors.[42]

The transformation of the Institute of Christian Virgins in Sichuan from a meditative group into an evangelizing force came with the arrival in 1772 of the French missionary Jean-Martin Moye (1730–1793) of the Missions Étrangères de Paris.[43] (Moye had just come from Europe, where he founded the Sisters of Divine Providence of Portieux in Lorraine, and he was convinced that women excelled men in spirituality.) Most of these Virgins came from prominent families, although they dedicated themselves to a life of austerity and service. In 1778 there was a severe famine in eastern Sichuan, and many starving peasants flocked to the city of Chongqing in search of food.[44] The officials established a camp for them half a league (approximately one and a half miles) outside of Chongqing and distributed rice there. Conditions at the camp were appalling, and epidemic diseases ravaged these people. So many people died that efforts to bury the corpses flagged, and the stench in the camp became foul. Moye, who was based at Chongqing, sent Christian Virgins to the camp to baptize moribund children. One of the most notable of these Virgins was Catherine Lo, who carefully compiled a catalog of the two thousand children she baptized.[45] It was her intention to use this catalog to follow up the baptisms with religious instruction, but when she later tried to find the children, she discovered that they had all died.

In April 1779 Moye sent some Christian Virgins to Hezhou (Hechuan). Missionaries tended to evaluate their efforts in terms of the number of baptisms. These women missionaries recorded two hundred baptisms on the way to Hezhou and a thousand in the city itself. These women faced great danger, but were inspired by the possibility of martyrdom. One Christian Virgin who baptized 1,500 children faced a dangerous situation when the sick child of a guard she baptized took a turn for the worse after being baptized. Aroused by the fact that all the children this Virgin had previously baptized had died, the father and a crowd of people feared that she was practicing some sort of witchcraft, and they threatened her life. They marched her to the magistrate, where she signed a statement in which she took responsibility for the child's life, although she told the crowd that it was really God who decided the child's fate. After the child survived for fifteen days, she was freed.

The Christian Virgins faced the danger of boat travel and the ever-present threat of brigands in the countryside in carrying their ministry long distances from Chongqing, supposedly making journeys of a hundred leagues (three hundred miles), traveling to the north and south of the city and even farther to the east. In his report to Propaganda, Moye claimed that thirty thousand children had been baptized in his mission district during the plague and famine years of 1778 and 1779. He appealed to Propaganda, saying that the zeal and unselfishness of the Virgins in baptizing moribund children in China needed to be supported with Europeans' financial contributions that would pay for the Virgins' subsistence.

In official documents, the Christian Virgins were referred to as "chaste women" (*tongzhen* or *zhennü*). Less formally, they were called "those who live in their parents' home" (*zhujiade*) and "old mothers" (*guniang*). The Sichuan rules for Christian Virgins were applied to all of China in 1832, and the Institute of Christian Virgins continued to function until the mid-twentieth century.

Some of the Christian Virgins combated infanticide as midwives. In 1846, the Jesuit superior in China, Fr. Claude Gotteland, obtained the cooperation of a Christian Virgin midwife in the effort to save children. The midwife agreed that when she was told to drown a newborn, she would instead bring the infant to Gotteland, who would baptize it and provide care for it.[46] Around 1842 the Lazarists in Beijing succeeded in placing a Christian Virgin in a public orphanage in Beijing. This enabled them to baptize large numbers of dying infants.[47]

NINETEENTH-CENTURY CATHOLIC EFFORTS

Because female infanticide was caused not only by practical problems like poverty, but also by cultural values and personal morality, nineteenth-century Christian missionaries realized that dealing with poverty alone would not eliminate infanticide. However, they found enormous resistance among many Chinese to their culturally insensitive and condescending presentation of the Christian message.

Chinese resistance was heightened by the abrasive manner of the later European Jesuits. The pioneering missionary work of the Jesuits in Jiangnan dated back to Francesco Brancati (Pan Guoguang), who worked there from 1623 until 1655 and developed a close pastoral relationship with the Xu family. After the Society of Jesus was dissolved in 1773, former Jesuits continued to serve in Jiangnan as secular priests until their deaths. Chinese Catholics remembered these last Jesuits as being devoted martyrs to their faith and pastors attentive to the needs of their Chinese flocks. Over the years, Jiangnan Catholics grew nostalgic for the Jesuits' return.

For fifty years the church in Jiangnan was served mainly by Chinese priests, many of whom were Lazarists, and administered by native Chinese laypeople. In 1834 the Catholics of the Jiangnan mission sent a petition to the pope, lamenting the neglected pastoral conditions in their mission and requesting the Jesuits' return.[48] In the following years, a second appeal, signed by fifty-one Catholic lay leaders of the Jiangnan church, was sent to the pope. Pope Gregory XVI responded favorably and the first contingent of new Jesuits arrived in 1842 in Shanghai. Jiangnan was turned over to the Jesuits and the Lazarist priests were forced to leave.

Unfortunately, the French Jesuits who arrived in 1842 were quite different from the former Jesuits. Facing a hostile atmosphere in postrevolutionary France, the French Jesuits had become defensive and rigid, unlike their earlier, accommodating confreres. Consequently, it took only five years for the Jiangnan Catholics to become disillusioned with the new Jesuits. They became even more disillusioned with Bishop Bési (Ludovicus, count of Bési), an arrogant aristocrat who achieved his clerical status through his connections with important people like Gregory XVI. Bési's administration was a disaster in China; he had a particularly contentious dispute with the Christian Virgins of Songjiang, who resisted his attempts to control their chanting in church. On Ash Wednesday 1846 the Jiangnan Catholics produced a thirty-eight-page open letter filled with their complaints about the abuse of authority by Bési and the Jesuits.[49]

Many families abandoned their newborn infants out of poverty on Chongming, a remote island at the mouth of the Yangzi River, just north of Shanghai. In April 1845 Fr. Stanislas Clavelin was sent to Chongming to minister to the long-neglected Christian community there. Europeans had never lived on the island, and Chongming was so remote and Clavelin's language skills so undeveloped that he asked the Jesuit superior Claude Gotteland to send him elsewhere. Gotteland refused, so Clavelin made the isolated trek by boat to Chongming, where he spent the first year as the sole missionary, replacing the Chinese Lazarist fathers

André Yang and Paul Cheng.[50] The first Jesuit sent to assist him could not endure the harsh conditions and his health forced him to withdraw. He was replaced in 1846 by the Jesuit Théobald Werner, newly arrived from France.

Clavelin was filled with enthusiasm for this ministry, and during his first six months there baptized more than six hundred moribund children. He secured the assistance of a non-Christian midwife who baptized eight hundred children. However, because most of the children they baptized died, the suspicion grew among the populace that the rite of baptism involved some sort of black magic that killed the children. Sometimes the baptizers were attacked with blows and stone throwing. In the desperate conditions of Chongming, newborn infants were available for sale for only 200–300 copper cash (4–5 French francs). The low cost was within the range of even poor Christian families who bought the children out of religious obligation and raised them as members of their families. Sometimes Christian Virgins bought the children to save them from being drowned.

But even in Chongming, infanticide was not limited to the poor. Werner wrote in 1852 of a wealthy non-Christian family in which the mother ordered that her newborn daughter be thrown in the dustbin to die.[51] When a Christian woman asked the mother for permission to retrieve the child from the dustbin and feed it, the mother refused on the grounds that the European priests would use the child's cadaver to make opium. Then the Christian woman asked if she might at least baptize the child, and the mother finally agreed only after being urged by other non-Christian women. After almost two days in the dustbin, the child uttered a long and painful wail and died.

After 1846, Catholic missionaries in China were able to duplicate aspects of the European institutional response to infant abandonment. They established Catholic orphanages throughout China with funds supplied by the Holy Childhood. The Holy Childhood began distributing funds in 1845 with 19,500 francs going mainly to China.[52] In 1846, 42,000 francs were sent to China alone. The funds going to China increased each year, and this probably accounts for many of the 101 orphanages established between 1847 and 1870 that are listed by Palatre.[53] Thirty-five of these were for girls, twenty were for boys, and the remainder contained mixed sexes of unspecified proportions.

The Congrégation des Missions Étrangères (Paris) ran thirty-four orphanages spread throughout the southwestern provinces of Sichuan, Guizhou, Yunnan, and Guangdong, and the northeastern province of Manchuria. One of the orphanages for girls in Manchuria was directed by the Sisters of Divine Providence of Portieux. Eleven of these were for girls and ten for boys, two were farm orphanages, and the others were not identified. Three of the orphanages in Guizhou (one for children under four years and two for boys) were ceded to the missionaries by the Chinese government in 1864.

The Dominicans ran two orphanages for girls in Fujian. The Franciscans ran twelve orphanages, including three in Shandong, two in Hunan (one of which was taken by the Chinese government in 1848 or 1849), two in Hubei (the Hankou orphanage for girls was directed by the Canossian Sisters), three in Shanxi, one in Shaanxi, and one in remote Gansu. Four of these were for girls, two were for boys, and the others were not identified by occupants. The Lazarists ran twenty-six orphanages in the most urban areas of China, which included Zhili (including Beijing), Jiangxi, and Zhejiang. Eleven of these were for girls and six were for boys, and one was a farm orphanage. Two of the orphanages in Beijing, one in Ningbo and one in Tinghaitin (?), were directed by the Sisters of Saint Vincent de Paul. The Congregation of Foreign Missions of Milan ran four orphanages in Henan. The Jesuits ran thirteen orphanages, including two at Zikawei. The girls' orphanage at Zikawei was directed by the Religious Auxiliaries of Purgatory.

In 1865 in Inner Mongolia, a new Belgian order, the Scheut Fathers, or CICM (Congregation Immaculati Cordis Mariae), became active in China mission work. The founder, Theopheil Verbiest, was the chaplain to the Holy Childhood in Belgium, and the Scheut fathers used the Holy Childhoood support from Europe to gather abandoned infants and care for them in orphanages. Palatre lists six Scheut orphanages in Mongolia. Two of them were in Xiwanzi (now called Chongli and located in Hebei Province); one of these was a farm orphanage.[54]

Abandoned infants brought to the Scheut missions in the Ordos (southwest) region of Inner Mongolia were baptized and given to either wet nurses (naima) or Catholic families.[55] Only two-thirds, and sometimes less than one-half, of the infants left at these Holy Childhood hospices survived. Small financial incentives were offered to help in the gathering of abandoned children. For each child brought to the mission, a beggar was rewarded two hundred copper cash and one measure of spiked millet (gumi); an itinerant physician was given free medicine, travel money, and a bonus. The mission recorded the name of the beggar and the names and address of the parents. However, the Tianjin Incident had served as a cautionary tale of Chinese sensitivity to gathering children, and after the Boxer Rebellion (1900), the finding fees were reduced or discontinued. The wet nurses were paid a monthly stipend of "mother's milk copper cash" (naizi qian) and yearly rations of cotton cloth and wadding. Children were weaned and returned to the mission by wet nurses at the age of four or five and by the Catholic families at the age of five or six. Girls remained in the Holy Childhood orphanage until reaching marriageable age (fifteen or sixteen). In the interim they were supervised by Christian Virgins and isolated from the rest of the world. After 1900, the Scheut orphanage at Ershisiqingli consisted of 139 children, six Virgins, three aspirants, one servant, and a water carrier.

Although the common people valued the Holy Childhood's work in Inner Mongolia, there were some critics. The most notable of these was the Lazarist father Vincent Lebbe (Lei Mingyuan) (1877–1940), who led a movement to revive Matteo Ricci's accommodation of Christianity with Chinese culture. Lebbe appealed to Rome to limit French influence, which he regarded as harmful to the growth of Christianity in China. In the process, he sought to diminish the influence of French priests by building up a native Chinese clergy. Given that the Holy Childhood was so closely connected with French patronage, it is not surprising that Lebbe was critical of its work in Mongolia. He believed that the results of the Holy Childhood's work in Mongolia were not proportional to the effort expended. He claimed that the process failed to prepare the children, particularly the boys, to become good Christians. Lebbe recommended that the work of the Holy Childhood be augmented by a program of evangelization. While abandoned children should continue to be collected by the church, he noted that their numbers in Mongolia were "less numerous than is believed."[56] Lebbe was not the only one to claim that the incidence of infanticide was lower in Mongolia than in China, but there is a lack of statistical evidence to confirm the claim.

Catholic orphanages have a mixed legacy in China. They were charitable institutions that served the poorest classes and provided for children, mainly girls, who otherwise would not have survived. The boys were taught practical job skills and the girls were taught needlework and homemaking.[57] Most of these orphans became faithful Catholics. Nevertheless, Catholic orphanages gave rise to ugly rumors that continued to fester among a suspicious Chinese public long after the missionaries were evicted from China in 1951. The mythology of the orphanages blended with Chinese views of Western imperialism. The lingering effects of this ill will surfaced in 1973 during the Cultural Revolution's campaign against religion when a children's book was published in Shanghai with pictures of Catholic nuns beating Chinese children in an orphanage.[58]

7

+

Female Infanticide
in Modern China

The fall of the Qing dynasty and the collapse of the imperial system in China in 1911 did not bring about the end of female infanticide. The material and cultural causes of infanticide continued, but were transformed by modern technology. The availability of more complete quantitative demographic records, however, allows us to better assess the extent of female infanticide in China.

The continuities with the past are apparent in the arrival of the first Maryknoll priests in China. When the Maryknollers arrived in Yeungkong (Yangjiang) in Guangdong Province in 1918, they found that the town orphanage did not accept infants or sick children. Consequently, they opened orphanages for abandoned babies in 1920 in Yeungkong and Luoding.[1] Like earlier missionaries, the Maryknoll priests paid a few cents for each abandoned baby brought to the orphanages. The reasons for the abandonment of children seem to have been quite similar to those of earlier times, and not all the infants came from poor families. Fr. Daniel Leo McShane remembered one infant girl who had been born in an unlucky month to a wealthy non-Christian family and who was given to the orphanage because of the family's fear that they would suffer if they raised her.[2]

Because of the priests' inability to manage the orphanages, five Maryknoll Sisters arrived in Yeungkong in 1922. The Sisters hired wet nurses to nurse and care for the babies in their homes for a monthly salary equivalent to one U.S. dollar. Every ten days the babies were brought back to the orphanage for a checkup. In 1924 four Sisters were sent to the orphanage in Luoding. When the Sisters in both Luoding and Yeungkong had to withdraw until 1930 to the safety of Hong Kong because of antiforeign demonstrations, their orphanage work was continued by Catholic ladies and Virgins. After 1930 the Sisters returned and the number of orphans expanded, although they consisted almost entirely of girls, many of whom were blind.

In 1927 the Nationalist government issued a regulation prohibiting the drowning of girls.[3] Article 284 of the 1928 Criminal Law (*Zhonghua Minguo jin xingfa*) provided punishment for mothers who killed their newborn children, but only if the children were illegitimate. This law was revised in the Republican Penal Code of 1935 to cover the killing of all newborn children, whether legitimate or illegitimate. In such cases, the mother was to be subject to imprisonment from six months to five years.

The Second Sino-Japanese War created a flood of abandonments, causing the annual baptisms of abandoned babies in Yeungkong to increase from 450 before 1937 to 731 in 1940, and from 1,000 to 2,500 in Luoding in the years 1937–1942.[4] Unfortunately, the condition of the abandoned babies was so poor that Maryknollers were able to save only 3–6 percent of all babies brought to them. These dismal numbers compared with other Catholic orphanages in China, where, in 1935, 299,000 abandoned babies were baptized in 365 orphanages. Apparently most of them died, since the orphanages housed only 28,900 orphans.

Female infanticide and neglect due to the earlier weaning of girls was probably responsible for the skewed sex ratios at birth recorded in the Republican period (1912–1949).[5] These practices were particularly notable in Guangdong, Guangxi, Henan, and Anhui provinces. The data for the 1930s and 1940s hint at an excess female infant mortality in the range of 10–15 percent. Although these percentages dropped sharply following the end of the Pacific War in 1945 and even further after the establishment of the People's Republic of China in 1949, approximately 2 percent of girls were missing throughout the 1960s and early 1970s. Even before ultrasound machines and sex-selective abortions became available on a massive scale in the mid-1980s, the percentage of missing girls increased to almost 5 percent, although it is difficult to say exactly what roles infanticide, abandonment, neglect, and adoption played.

After the Communists came to power, the Marriage Law of 1950 strictly prohibited infanticide by drowning and other methods. Mao Zedong had encouraged large families and it was not until after Mao's death that Deng Xiaoping was able to address the problem of China's overpopulation. However, the one-child birth-control program beginning in 1979 introduced policies and technology that intensified the traditional Chinese preference for male children and revived drowning and other forms of female infanticide. As a consequence, male-to-female sex ratios become increasingly imbalanced. Birth-control planners in Beijing failed to anticipate the ferociousness and even savagery of the reaction of peasants to this attempt to impede their desire for sons.[6] This led to a series of brutally coercive government campaigns where pregnant women were reported to have been detained in cells, coerced by mass rallies into having abortions, and even escorted to surgical areas by armed personnel. Sometimes husbands reacted violently by killing government officials and were, in turn, executed.

The situation was exacerbated by the banning of minor marriages; the ban eliminated this more benign form of abandonment. In urbanized provinces like Jiangsu, where implementation was stricter, the bodies of infant girls were found in rivers, fields, and public lavatories.[7] Surveys made by *People's Daily* reported that most of the abandoned, maimed, and murdered children were infant girls and that in some district orphanages, infant girls made up 99 percent of the total number of orphans. It appears that the reemergence of female infanticide was concentrated in the poorer inland regions, such as Hubei and Hunan provinces, where infanticide had been a traditional practice that was rarely viewed as a crime.[8]

The sensitivity of the Chinese government to female infanticide was revealed in the highly publicized case of Steven Westley Mosher, which featured a dramatic mix of coercive Chinese birth-control policies, debatable professional behavior on Mosher's part, a defensive Chinese government, the revenge of his spurned Chinese wife, and a questionable reaction by a leading American university. Mosher was a Fresno, California, native who, after graduating with bachelor's and master's degrees from the University of Washington in 1973, was commissioned in the U.S. Navy and stationed in East Asia. There he met and married Maggie So, a Hong Kong Chinese. In 1976 he entered Stanford University and enrolled in their doctoral program in anthropology.[9]

In 1979 Mosher went to Taiwan to do dissertation research. He received a grant from the now-defunct American Committee on Scholarly Communication with the People's Republic of China and at the age of thirty-four became one of the first American scholars to do field research in China. In March 1979 he began one year of residence at Sandhead Brigade, a pseudonym for a village in Shunde County in southern Guandong Province. The fact that this was the native village of Mosher's Chinese father-in-law enabled him to gain access to it as the spouse of an "overseas Chinese" villager. Over the next year, Mosher's proficiency in Cantonese and interaction with the villagers gave him information about how the repressive policies of China's birth-control program forced village women into abortions at advanced stages (seventh and eight months) of pregnancy.

Meanwhile, Mosher's marriage to Maggie So was disintegrating. She had her own professional plans and in March 1980, she visited Mosher in her ancestral village, where she had cousins. After a bitter quarrel,

Mosher demanded a divorce. His wife is said to have resisted and threatened to ruin him. She went to the American consulate in Canton and accused him of bribing local officials to obtain confidential documents. In
May 1981, when Mosher published an article in a Taiwanese magazine
featuring photographs of young women undergoing forced late-term
abortions, the mainland Chinese government was outraged. In December
1981 Mosher's wife repeated her accusations to Mosher's professors at
Stanford. The Stanford Anthropology Department, denying any pressure
from Beijing, voted in 1983 to expel him from the doctoral program for
unprofessional conduct. This decision aroused an international controversy over academic freedom and the abortion policies of mainland
China.[10]

In his 1983 book, *Broken Earth*, Mosher argued that rural women in
Guangdong were subject to more than forced abortions. He claimed that
female infanticide had recently reappeared in rural China after a long absence, as a result of harsh birth-control policies. He wrote:

> On my frequent trips to Hong Kong, after leaving China, I began to hear re-
> ports of female infanticide from Chinese friends who had made trips back to
> Pearl River Delta Commune. That the "one child per family" policy is re-
> sponsible for this brutal practice there can be no doubt.[11]

In a 1999 interview, Mosher described a form of infanticide used in
South China hospitals during his residence there in 1979–1980.[12] At birth,
when a woman's cervix was completely dilated and the baby's head
emerged from descending the birth canal, the physician would inject
formaldehyde, alcohol, or iodine into the baby's brain, causing instanta-
neous death and a stillbirth. Mosher compared the procedure to a "partial-
birth abortion" (intact dilation and extraction procedure). He claimed that
during an interview in South China, the head of a large military hospital
claimed that his procedure was technically not infanticide because it was
legal to take a baby's life as long as part of a foot was still in the womb.
At that time, the physician claimed to be doing about four hundred such
procedures each year.

Although Mosher's confrontational tone diminishes his credibility as a
scholar, he is not the only one to have seen a link between China's strict
birth-control policies and the resurgence of female infanticide. The Chinese government has explained infanticide as the continuation of a feudal
practice that is outdated in modern China and blamed it on the superstition of the peasants. However, the resurgence of infanticide was caused as
much by contemporary practical concerns as by a clinging to old traditions. Since the government does not provide retirement benefits, parents
depend on their sons to support them in their old age. In this concern,

daughters are viewed as "lost" because they will be absorbed into their husbands' families. A Guangdong Province newspaper reported that most of the two hundred female infants who died in the fall of 1982 were victims of infanticide.[13] Following the parents' instructions, the midwife had a bucket of water ready and if a girl was born, she drowned it immediately. Officially, the death was reported as a stillbirth.[14] Most of the infanticides today apparently occur in remote villages where women give birth at home and where the midwife is probably a neighbor and relative. All of this is remarkably evocative of nineteenth-century practices.

The story of infanticide in contemporary China is complicated by moral and political considerations involving current governmental policies. In 1990, a controversial book by a retired U.S. government worker and China-population specialist named John S. Aird appeared. The title, *Slaughter of the Innocents,* was an allusion to the biblical slaughter of male children by King Herod, but was applied to the contemporary Chinese policies on birth control. The book is more political than scholarly and defends the American policy of withholding funding from the United Nations Population Fund on the grounds of the coercive nature of China's birth-control policies. An appendix on infanticide describes unconfirmed reports of infanticide by obstetricians in urban Chinese hospitals involving children who have been born without official authorization.[15] The reported cases of infanticide involved injecting formaldehyde or alcohol into the baby's head, smashing the skull with forceps as the baby emerged from the birth canal, stuffing gauze into the infant's mouth, and strangulation. The physicians were said to be compelled by government authorities to destroy these infants as part of China's birth-control program.

The one-child policy was applied with regional variations: It was applied more strictly in urban areas than in rural areas, where resistance was stronger. Implementation tightened in the late 1980s when the one-child policy was modified to a "one-son/two-child policy." If the first child was a son, no further children were allowed, but if it was a girl, the family was allowed to have a second child in the hopes of having a boy. The tightening of the previously lax oversight with this new birth-control policy in rural areas caused a measurable spike in the abandonment of girls, who were mainly second-born daughters.[16] Although the one-child policy played an important role in skewing the sex ratios in China, it was not the only factor involved. Other Asian countries without a one-child policy—notably Taiwan, South Korea, and India—experienced a similar imbalance in sex ratios during the 1980s and 1990s. The availability of inexpensive new technology in the form of ultrasound scanners and sex-selective abortions all played a significant role.[17] More recently, social and political changes in South Korea have created a more positive attitude toward female babies. This has caused a shift in the sex ratio at birth from 116.5 boys born for every 100 girls in 1990 to 107.4 boys per 100 girls in 2006.[18]

Certain elements in contemporary infanticide echo those of earlier centuries. One of these elements involves the role of orphanages. In the early 1990s, China's orphanages began to be flooded with increasing numbers of abandoned female infants.[19] Moreover, up to half of these female infants died during the first few months after arrival. This was reminiscent of the high death rates in the foundling hospices of earlier centuries and reflects the inadequacies of trying to care for infants in an institutionalized setting, regardless of the country or the period.

Overcrowded conditions in orphanages led foreign groups to make serious accusations of child abuse. In 1995 three British filmmakers posing as charity workers entered Chinese orphanages carrying a concealed camera to investigate rumors of high death rates among children.[20] In a state-run orphanage in Guangdong Province they found a skeletal, malnourished baby girl named Mei Ming (literally, "no name"). In July 1995 they broadcast their findings on Channel Four in Britain in a thirty-eight-minute television documentary entitled *The Dying Rooms*.[21] The film was rebroadcast in the United States on January 24, 1996, on Cinemax. The film accused the orphanage staff of deliberately choosing to let Mei Ming die and then placing her in a "dying room" ten days before the film crew inadvertently discovered her.

The broadcast of *The Dying Rooms* was followed in early 1996 by a 331-page indictment from Human Rights Watch, an advocacy group in New York, accusing China's child-welfare system of the starvation, abuse, and neglect of children in its care. The report was based largely on the testimony of Zhang Shuyun, a Chinese physician who had served on the staff of the Shanghai Children's Welfare Institute before leaving China in March 1995. She alleged that thousands of children in China had died in the same manner as Mei Ming. These accusers have not been without their critics. The Chinese foreign ministry denied the existence of such "dying rooms," and the government responded with a counterdocumentary entitled *The Dying Rooms: A Patchwork of Lies*, in which it claimed that Mei Ming was actually a boy. Many American parents who had adopted Chinese girls defended the Chinese government and were vocal in claiming that the *The Dying Rooms* and Human Rights Watch had exaggerated abusive conditions in China.[22] In the aftermath of these charges, the Chinese Ministry of Civil Affairs closed orphanages to all outsiders and to most Chinese.

Although detailed data is available from censuses (1953, 1964, 1982, 1990, and 2000) and fertility surveys, one can only speculate about the unreported births of girls due to deaths very early in life.[23] In the 1990s, the number of missing girls amounted to almost one million annually.[24] The

ratio of almost 119 boys born for every 100 girls in China in 2005 compared to a worldwide average of 105 boys for 100 girls.[25] On the basis of
these ratios, it is projected that by the year 2020 there will be thirty million
more men than women in the twenty-to-forty-five age group. Of course,
a deficiency of marriageable women has frequently been a problem in
Chinese history. Determining the extent of female infanticide has been
complicated by the emergence of sex-selective abortions as the primary
means of getting rid of unwanted girls. Ethnic differences and educational
level account for some of the distorted sex ratios.[26] A preference for sons
is greatest among the Han-Chinese majority and the Zhuang and Manchu
ethnic groups. The sex ratios are normal among Muslim groups in north-
western China, and there is a preponderance of infant girls among the Ti-
betans. Clearly this is not just a matter of peasant superstition. Families
with a higher level of education report a greater proportion of missing
girls because better schooling enables families to practice more effective
sex screening through sex-selective abortions.

Nevertheless, it is unclear how many of these "missing girls" have been
eliminated through infanticide and abortion and how many of them are
simply "hidden" through informal adoptions and foster care.[27] Many girls
were never registered at birth and are known as "black children" (*hei
haize*). These girls are believed to be living secretly with their parents in
their native villages, while local officials tolerate or remain unaware of the
child's actual relationship to her caregivers.

In 1979, when the "one-child policy" was being introduced in China,
the Chinese manufactured their first ultrasound machine. Although ultrasound machines were intended for the diagnosis of health problems,
including fetal defects, they are also capable of determining the sex of the
embryo. Since 1979, large numbers of imported and locally made ultrasound machines have been put into use, so by 1990 it was estimated that
one hundred thousand ultrasound scanners were operating in China.[28]
Although it has been illegal since 1987 to tell parents the sex of a child de-
tected by an ultrasound machine, the law has been frequently violated, often for a bribe consisting of a mere carton of cigarettes.[29]

Throughout Chinese history, regional variations have made it difficult
to generalize from one region to the entire nation, and this remains true
today. In March 2003 the police in Guangxi Province detained a long-
distance bus holding twenty-eight baby girls being shipped for sale in Anhui Province, a thousand miles to the north.[30] The girls had been swathed
in quilts and stuffed in groups of two to four in plastic bags and packed
into the back of the bus. They were blue from lack of oxygen and one had
died from suffocation. The girls were between two and five months old
and had been sold by poor farmers to a baby trafficker in Yulin. Unlike in
other areas, such as neighboring Guangdong Province, in Guangxi the

one-child policy was still strictly enforced, and this caused poor farmers to sell their daughters in hopes of having a son. The births of these girls were probably never registered because poor women often receive no prenatal care.

What is saving these girls from abortions and infanticide is the demand for girls in other areas of China as well as in foreign countries. Childless city dwellers who have pensions to support them in their old age show a slight preference for girls, who they believe are more likely than boys to care for aging parents. Other girls are sold to rural families who want a daughter to help with housework. Others are sold as child brides for farmers in remote areas. The irony of this situation is that while the pool of available brides is limited and their value enhanced through their scarcity, some rural families continue, as in the past, to abort female fetuses and to abandon newborn girls.[31]

By 1990 the Chinese government's resistance to the adoption of Chinese children by non-Asians began to weaken.[32] In 1989, only 201 Chinese children were adopted by American parents through informal procedures. This began to change when a 1991 law relieved restrictions on foreign adoptions while severely limiting domestic adoptions. Because of birth-control policies, adoptions within China were restricted to childless couples over thirty-five years of age, and there was an effort to prevent parents from changing a daughter's registration status to "adopted" in order to try again for a son.[33] In an attempt to relieve the bulging orphanages, restrictions on foreign adoption were eased, giving foreigners the right to adopt Chinese children. The number of Chinese children (overwhelmingly girls) adopted by American parents reached 7,906 in the year ending September 30, 2005, before dropping in the face of additional restrictions imposed by the Chinese on foreign adoptions.[34]

Pressure emerged in the 1989 United Nations' Convention on the Rights of the Child and the 1993 Hague Conference's Convention on Protection of Children and Cooperation in Respect of Intercountry Adoption. Both conventions argued that moral concerns should give domestic adoption priority over international adoption. Although the domestic adoption law was revised in 1999, pressure from birth-control programs and vested interests that were profiting from international adoptions limited the revisions.[35] In 2008 the government in Beijing announced that it was considering incremental changes that would loosen its strict population policies.[36]

Christianity in China today is a resurgent force that continues the battle against female infanticide, except that there have been no missionaries in China since 1951. The baptism of infants is no longer an issue because the Communist government forbids baptism before the age of eighteen.[37]

Although the Catholic Church in China remains divided between the government-sanctioned church and a Vatican-sanctioned underground church, in 1989 Bishop Zong Huaide, chairman of the government-sponsored China Patriotic Catholic Association, referred to their common ground on this issue. He said, "What we really are against is female infanticide. That is a big sin."[38]

8

✛

Conclusion

The heart of the controversy over female infanticide in China lies in the defensive feelings evoked by the horror and shame over the killing of helpless infant girls. The long history of female infanticide in China raises the possibility of something intrinsic in Chinese culture or the Chinese people that causes these brutal acts. In its most blatant form, this insensitivity to life is seen as a Chinese racial trait and evokes racism. Few people today believe in this type of racial stereotyping. However, there are other less blatant but also disquieting explanations involving the possibility of ethnic or cultural traits among the Chinese that generate this killing of little girls.

Viewed from a Chinese cultural perspective, the degree of homicide involved in the killing of girls at birth was lessened by the Chinese view that newborn infants had not yet fully attained human status and did so only gradually over time. Exactly how long this process took was debatable. Certain ceremonies marked this point of transition, such as the ancient ceremony in which a father would lift up (accept) or not lift up (reject) a three-day-old child; the latter action would force a mother to abandon a rejected child. A more benign ceremony marking this transition was the third-day bath. Consequently, drowning a child before that point was not regarded as murder to the same degree as killing a child after that time was. This is somewhat comparable to the viewpoint widely held (though highly contested) in the United States today that first- and second-trimester abortions (when the fetus is between one and six months old) are more acceptable than third-trimester abortions (when the fetus is between seven and nine months old). This reasoning is based largely on

127

the viability (ability to survive) of the premature child outside the mother's womb. The Chinese view was reinforced by their medical theories, which saw the development of a human being in terms of the gradual coming together of certain dispersed cosmic and biological forces after birth.

Another contributing cultural factor was Confucianism, which honored age over youth and males over females and so gave some degree of philosophical and moral justification to female infanticide. And yet, even Confucianism was divided on this issue and many literati quoted Mencius, a disciple of Confucius, to argue that killing girls was unnatural and immoral. The use of moral issues to justify infanticide might be compared to the contemporary worldwide invocation of a woman's right to choose in justifying abortion today. In China, a driving force in female infanticide was practical. Males could make a greater practical contribution to the family while females were a drain on the family's resources. Whatever was spent on raising a girl would be lost when she married and left the family. Moreover, her marriage would require a costly dowry that would further drain the family's resources. This might be compared to the quality-of-life argument that is made to justify aborting the children of poor and underage, single mothers in the world today.

Chinese were by no means unanimous in justifying the killing of children. Many Chinese had mixed feelings about female infanticide and many others opposed it vigorously. Some Chinese opposed infanticide on the grounds of basic human compassion. Others opposed it on religious grounds. Buddhism was a leading force in resisting infanticide because Buddhists were opposed to the killing of any sentient beings, which included animals as well as humans. Moreover, from the Buddhist perspective, a newborn child had fully developed human status because of the reincarnation process, and there was no distinction between killing a newborn infant and an elderly person.

In China the battle against infanticide has been waged for as long as it has been practiced. Although many historians have claimed that the Qing dynasty was a period of decline, Confucian paternalism fostered creative efforts by literati and gentry in the nineteenth century to develop infant protection societies. These societies attempted to combat infanticide by making financial contributions to poor families with newborn children and by organizing infant hospices with wet nurses to feed abandoned children.

The arrival of Christian missionaries in China introduced further opposition to infanticide on the religious grounds that because each individual was endowed with a soul and intrinsic worth at conception, killing a newborn infant was as wrong as killing any other human being. However, many Chinese, antagonized by Western imperialist insensitivity, were suspicious of Catholic efforts to collect and baptize moribund children, believing that the missionaries were using the children's bodies to produce medicinal substances. By the nineteenth century, the financial contributions of the Society of the Holy Childhood enabled the Catholic missionaries to open orphanages to save abandoned children. However, these Catholic orphanages competed with Chinese orphanages and offended Chinese cultural pride.

Female infanticide in China became such a compelling issue in the nineteenth century that it spilled over to the West to produce uniquely European controversies. Hostility toward Catholic priests in postrevolutionary republican France generated debate over the accusation that missionaries were exaggerating the extent of infanticide among the Chinese as a ploy to generate sympathy for Chinese children and increase contributions to Catholic mission funds. This debate extended to the mission field in China when newly arrived Protestant missionaries, acting out of ignorance, anti-Catholicism, and sympathy for the Chinese, initially doubted whether infanticide was extensive.

The practice of female infanticide ebbed and flowed with economic and social upheavals in Chinese history and was almost extinguished in the mid-twentieth century; however, it has returned in recent times in the form of sex-selective abortions. The Chinese government blamed the resurgence of female infanticide on the persistence of feudal ideas and peasant superstition, but the movement was caused largely by the strict birth-control policies instituted after 1979 and by new medical technology.

In addition to the practical side, complex moral issues are involved. This book has argued that this complexity can be understood by comparing the debate over female infanticide in China to our own great debate over abortion in the West. Sorting out these various elements involving female infanticide in China is just as complicated and controversial as sorting out the practical and moral elements involved in abortions in the United States today.

Once we begin to understand the dynamics of female infanticide in China, we can better appreciate the Chinese perspective and see the common practical, moral, and spiritual dimensions that mark this as a human rather than a Chinese problem. Ultimately, though, this is not about understanding, but about human compassion and suffering. And because of that ultimate concern and the dimensions involved (unknown millions of exterminated girls), the drowning of girls in China must be added to the other terrible forms of inhumanity that have left their mark and horror in world history.

Bibliography

Abeel, David. "Notices of Infanticide Collected from the People of Fukien." *Chinese Repository* 10 (October 1843): 540–48.

Aird, John S. [John Shields]. *Slaughter of the Innocents: Coercive Birth Control in China*. Washington, DC: AEI, 1990.

Annales de l'Oeuvre de la Sainte-Enfance. Paris, 1846–1982, 586 issues, 126 vols.

Annales de la Propagation de la Foi. Lyon, 1842 et seq.

Bangert, William V., SJ. *A History of the Society of Jesus*. Rev. ed. St. Louis: Institute of Jesuit Sources, 1986.

Bartoli, Daniello. *Dell'historia della Compagnia de Giesu. La Cina, terca parte dell'Asia*. Rome, 1663.

Berkelbach van der Sprenkel, Otto. "Genealogical Registers." In *Essays on the Sources for Chinese History*, edited by Donald D. Leslie, Colin Mackerras, and Wang Gungwu, 83–98. Canberra: Australian National University Press, 1973.

Birrell, Anne. *Chinese Mythology: An Introduction*. Baltimore: Johns Hopkins University Press, 1999.

Boswell, John. *The Kindness of Strangers: The Abandonment of Children in Western Europe from Late Antiquity to the Renaissance*. Chicago: University of Chicago Press, 1988.

Bradshaw, Sue, OSF. "Catholic Sisters in China." In *Women in China: Current Directions in Historical Scholarship*, edited by Richard W. Guisso and Stanley Johannesen, 201–13. Youngstown, NY: Philo, 1981.

Bridgman, Elijah Coleman. "Infanticide, as Described in a Proclamation . . . Dated February 19th 1838." *Chinese Repository* 7, no. 1 (May 1838): 54–56.

———. Review of *China: Its State and Prospects, with Especial Reference to the Spread of the Gospel*, by W. H. Medhurst. *Chinese Repository* 9, no. 2 (June 1840): 74–83.

Britton, Roswell S. *The Chinese Periodical Press, 1800–1912*. Shanghai: Kelly & Walsh, 1933.

Broder, Sherri. *Tramps, Unfit Mothers, and Neglected Children: Negotiating the Family in Nineteenth-Century Philadelphia*. Philadelphia: University of Pennsylvania Press, 2002.

Chappet. "Rapport par le Docteur Chappet." *Bulletin de la Société de Géographie de Lyon* 5 (1884): 377–91.

Charbonnier, Jean-Pierre. *Christians in China: A.D. 600 to 2000*. Translated by M. N. L. Couve de Murville. San Francisco: Ignatius, 2007.

———. *Histoire des Chrétiens de Chine*. Paris: Desclée/Bégédis, 1992.

[Chavannes, E.?]. "Nécrologie. Charles Piton, 1835–1905." *T'oung Pao*, 2nd ser., 6 (1905): 508–9.

Chaves, Jonathan. "A Poem on Female Infanticide by Chiang Shih-ch'üan/Jiang Shiquan." *Sino-Western Cultural Relations Journal* 29 (2007): 1–4.

Ch'en, Kenneth K. S. *Buddhism in China: A Historical Survey*. Princeton, NJ: Princeton University Press, 1964.

Cihang pudu ce [Collection of the compassionate ship for passing through the Sea of the World]. Reprinted in Tongzhi reign, 1862–1874.

Coale, Ansley J., and Judith Banister. "Five Decades of Missing Females in China." *Proceedings of the American Philosophical Society* 140, no. 4 (December 1996): 421–50.

Cohen, Paul. *China and Christianity: The Missionary Movement and the Growth of Chinese Anti-Foreignism, 1860–1870*. Cambridge, MA: Harvard University Press, 1963.

Colombel, SJ. "Ch. VI. Le Kiang-nan." In *Les missions catholiques françaises au XIX siècle*, edited by Jean-Baptiste Piolet, 3: 161–231. Paris: Librairie Armand Colin, 1902.

Couling, Samuel. *The Encyclopedia Sinica*. Shanghai: Kelly & Walsh, 1917.

Couplet, Philippe, SJ. *Histoire d'une dame chrétienne de la Chine*. Paris, 1688.

Croll, Elizabeth J. *Endangered Daughters: Discrimination and Development in Asia*. London: Routledge, 2000.

Daojiao dazidian [Dictionary of the Daoist teaching]. Hangzhou: Zhejiang Guji Chubanshe, 1987.

Dennys, N. B."Shanghai. General Geographical Description, Etc." In *The Treaty Ports of China and Japan*, edited by William Frederick Mayers, N. B. Dennys, and Charles King, 350–413. London: Trübner, 1867.

Dudink, Ad. "The Chinese Christian Books of the Former Beitang Library." *Sino-Western Cultural Relations Journal* 26 (2004): 46–59.

Ebrey, Patricia Buckley. *The Inner Quarter*. Berkeley: University of California Press, 1993.

Edkins, Joseph. "A Sketch of the Taoist Mythology in Modern Form." *Journal of the North China Branch of the Royal Asiatic Society* 3 (1859): 309–14.

Eitel, Ernst Johann. "Notices of New Books." *China Review* 16 (July 1887–June 1888): 189–90.

Entenmann, Robert E. "Chinese Catholic Clergy and Catechists in Eighteenth-Century Szechuan." In *Actes du VIe Colloque internationale de Sinologie*, 389–410. Taipei: Ricci Institute, 1995.

———. "Christian Virgins in Eighteenth-Century Sichuan." In *Christianity in China from the Eighteenth Century to the Present*, edited by Daniel H. Bays, 180–93. Stanford, CA: Stanford University Press, 1996.

Evans, Karin. *The Lost Daughters of China*. New York: Penguin, 2000.

Fang Hao, *Zhongguo Tianzhujiao shi renwu chuan* [Biographies of historical personages in the Chinese Catholic Church]. 3 vols. Hong Kong: Gongjiao Renlixue Hui, 1970–73.

Fielde, Adele M. *Pagoda Shadows: Studies from Life in China*. Boston: W. G. Corthell, 1884.

Fogel, Joshua A., ed. *The Nanjing Massacre in History and Historiography*. Berkeley: University of California Press, 2000.

Fuchs, Rachel Ginnes. *Abandoned Children: Foundlings and Child Welfare in Nineteenth-Century France*. Albany: State University of New York Press, 1984.

Furth, Charlotte. "Concepts of Pregnancy, Childbirth, and Infancy in Ch'ing Dynasty China." *Journal of Asian Studies* 46 (1987): 7–35.

Gabet, J. *Un mot sur l'infanticide en Chine*. Liège, Belgium: H. Dessain, 1854.

Gaubil, Antoine, SJ. *Correspondance de Pékin, 1722–1759*. Edited by Renée Simon. Geneva: Librairie Droz, 1970.

Gernet, Jacques. *Daily Life in China on the Eve of the Mongol Invasion, 1250–1276*. Translated by H. M. Wright. Stanford, CA: Stanford University Press, 1962.

Giles, Herbert, organizer. "The Prevalence of Infanticide in China." *Journal of the North China Branch of the Royal Asiatic Society* 20 (1885): 25–50.

Golvers, Noël. "Western Sources." In *Handbook of Christianity in China*. Vol. 1, *635–1800*, edited by N. Standaert, 46–52. Leiden: Brill, 2001.

Goodrich, Anne Swann. *Chinese Hells*. St. Augustin, Germany: Monumenta Serica, 1981.

Greenhalgh, Susan, and Edwin A. Winckler. *Governing China's Population*. Stanford, CA: Stanford University Press, 2005.

Guobao tu [Illustrations of just rewards]. One of 4 vols. that compose *Zhuyu yuan* [The round pearl]. Shanghai, n.d.

Handlin Smith, Joanna F. "Benevolent Societies: The Reshaping of Charity during the Late Ming and Early Ch'ing." *Journal of Asian Studies* 46 (1987): 309–36.

Ho, Ping-ti. *Studies on the Population of China, 1368–1953*. Cambridge, MA: Harvard University Press, 1959.

Ho-tong-tse. *Zhengying baoying lu* [Record of rewards for those who save children]. Reprint, 1869.

Hom, Sharon K. "Female Infanticide in China: The Human Rights Specter and Thoughts towards (An)other Vision." *Columbia Human Rights Law Review* 23 (1992): 249–314.

Huang Zhiwei. "Xujiahui Cangshulou" [The Xujiahui (Zi-ka-wei) Library]. English translation by Norman Walling, SJ. *Tripod* (July–August 1992): 22–35.

Huc, E. *Souvenirs d'un voyage dans la Tartarie et le Thibet pendant les années 1844, 1845 et 1846*. 2 vols. Paris, 1850.

Hui Qinglou, "'Deyi lu' banben kao lun" [An investigation into the editions of the *Deyi lu*]. *Nankai xuebao (Zhexue shehui kexue ban)* 11 (2006): 126–31.

Huibao (Shanghai newspaper).

Hummel, Arthur, ed. *Eminent Chinese of the Ch'ing Period*. Washington, DC: U.S. Government Printing Office, 1943.

Jennes, Jos, CICM. *Four Centuries of Catechetics in China*. English translation by Albert Van Lierde, Chinese translation by T'ien Yung-cheng, CICM. Taipei: Tianzhujiao Huaming Shuju, 1976.

Jiangnan tielei tu xin bian [The misfortunes of Jiangnan with illustrations—new edition]. Suzhou, n.d.

Jie ninü tushuo [An illustrated warning against drowning girls]. N.p., n.d.

"Jie ninü wen" [Exhortation against drowning girls]. Preface to *An shi deng zhujie* [Commentary on the lamp in the dark house]. Suzhou, 1849.

Jiuying xinchang [Saving young girls—new edition]. Wuchang ed. N.p., 1873.

Johnson, Kay Ann. *Wanting a Daughter, Needing a Son: Abandonment, Adoption, and Orphanage Care in China*. St. Paul, MN: Yeong & Yeong, 2004.

Johnson, Kay et al. "Infant Abandonment and Adoption in China." *Population and Development Review* 24, no. 3 (September 1998): 469–510.

Kern, H., trans. *Saddharma-Pundarika, or The Lotus of the True Law*. Oxford: Clarendon, 1884.

Kertzer, David I. *Sacrificed for Honor: Italian Infant Abandonment and the Politics of Reproductive Control*. Boston: Beacon, 1993.

King, Gail. "Candida Xu and the Growth of Christianity in China in the Seventeenth Century," *Monumenta Serica* 46 (1998): 49–66.

———. "The Xujiahui (Zikawei) Library of Shanghai." *Libraries and Culture* 32, no. 4 (1997): 456–69.

King, Marjorie. *China's American Daughter: Ida Pruitt (1888–1985)*. Hong Kong, 2006.

Kingston, Maxine Hong. *The Woman Warrior: Memoirs of a Girlhood among Ghosts*. New York: Knopf, 1977.

Kinney, Anne Behnke. *Representations of Childhood and Youth in Early China*. Stanford, CA: Stanford University Press, 2004.

Langer, William L. "Infanticide: A Historical Survey." *History of Childhood Quarterly* 1 (1973): 353–65; 2 (1974): 129–34.

Latourette, Kenneth Scott. *A History of Christian Missions*. London: Society for Promoting Christian Knowledge, 1929.

Lauwaert, Françoise. *Le meurtre en famille. Parricide et infanticide en Chine (XVIIe–XIXe siècles)*. Paris: Éditions Odile Jacob, 1999.

Lee, Bernice J. "Female Infanticide in China." In *Women in China: Current Directions in Historical Scholarship*, 163–77. Youngstown, NY: Philo, 1981.

Lee, James Z., and Cameron D. Campbell. *Fate and Fortune in Rural China: Social Organization and Population Behavior in Liaoning, 1774–1873*. Cambridge, UK: Cambridge University Press, 1997.

Lee, James Z., and Wang Feng. *One Quarter of Humanity: Malthusian Mythology and Chinese Realities*. Cambridge, MA: Harvard University Press, 1999.

Legge, James, trans. *The Chinese Classics*. 5 vols. Oxford: Oxford University Press, 1893.

———. *Li Chi—Book of Rites*. In *Sacred Books of the East*. Vols. 27–28. Oxford: Oxford University Press, 1885.

Lettres édifiantes et curieuses de Chine par des missionnaires Jésuites, 1702–1776. Edited by Isabelle and Jean-Louis Vissière. Paris: Garnier-Flammarion, 1979.

Lettres édifiantes et curieuses écrites des missions etrangères par quelques missionnaires de la Compagnie de Jésus. 34 vols. Paris: Nicolas Le Clerc, 1702–1776. New ed. edited by M. L. Aimé-Martin. 4 vols. Paris: Société du Panthéon littéraire, 1843.

Leung, Angela Ki Che. "L'accueil des enfants abandonnés dans la Chine du Bas-Yangzi aux XVIIe et XVIIIe siècles." *Études chinoises* 4 (1985): 15–54.

———. "Relief Institutions for Children in Nineteenth-Century China." In *Chinese Views of Childhood*, edited by Anne Behnke Kinney, 251–78. Honolulu: University of Hawaii Press, 1995.

Leys, Simon [Pierre Ryckmans]. *The Burning Forest: Essays on Chinese Culture and Politics*. New York: Henry Holt, 1986.

Li Jiugong. *Shensi lu* [Record of careful reflections]. In *Yesuhui Luoma danganguan Ming-Qing Tianzhujiao wenxian*, edited by Nicolas Standaert and Adrian Dudink, 9: 119–238. Taipei: Ricci Institute, 2002.

Li, Lillian M. "Life and Death in a Chinese Famine: Infanticide as a Demographic Consequence of the 1935 Yellow River Flood." *Comparative Studies in Society and History* 33 (1991): 466–510.

Liang-ki-koei [Liang Qigui?]. *Xuetang riji* [Diary for schools]. Suzhou ed. 1860.

Lin Yutang, *The Gay Genius: The Life and Times of Su Tungpo*. New York: John Day, 1947.

Loewe, Michael, ed. *Early Chinese Texts: A Bibliographical Guide*. Berkeley: Society for the Study of Early China, 1993.

Lowe, H. L. [Lu Xingyuan]. *The Adventures of Wu*. 2 vols. Beijing: Peking Chronicle Press, 1940–41.

Lutz, Jessie G. "Mission Dilemmas: Bride Price, Minor Marriage, Concubinage, Infanticide, and Education of Women." New Haven, CT: Yale Divinity School Library Occasional Publication no. 16, 2002.

Macgowan, D. J. "Prevalence of Infanticide in China." *China Review* (Hong Kong) 14 (July 1885–June 1886): 205–8.

Mann, Susan. "Grooming a Daughter for Marriage: Brides and Wives in the Mid-Ch'ing Period." In *Marriage and Inequality in Chinese Society*, edited by Rubie S. Watson and Patricia Buckley Ebrey, 204–30. Berkeley: University of California Press, 1991.

———. *Precious Records: Women in China's Long Eighteenth Century*. Stanford, CA: Stanford University Press, 1997.

Mayer, Hans Eberhard. *The Crusades*. Translated by John Gillingham. New York: Oxford University Press, 1972.

McDonagh, Joseph. *Child Murder and British Culture, 1720–1900*. Cambridge, UK: Cambridge University Press, 2003.

McGreal, Leo F., SJ, et al. *Portraits of China*. Shanghai: Tou-se-wei Press, 1936.

McManus, John F. "Interview with Steven W. Mosher." *New America* 15, no. 8 (April 12, 1999): 21–23.

Mendoza, Juan Gonzalez de. *Historia de las cosas mas notables, ritos y costumbres, del gran Reyno de China*. Rome, 1585.

Menegon, Eugenio. "Ancestors, Virgins, and Friars: The Localization of Christianity in Late Imperial Mindong (Fujian, China), 1632–1863." PhD diss., University of California, Berkeley, 2002.

———. "Christian Loyalists, Spanish Friars, and Holy Virgins in Fujian during the Ming-Qing Transition." *Monumenta Serica* 51 (2003): 335–65.

Mirsky, Jonathan. "The Infanticide Tragedy in China." *Nation* 237, no. 1 (July 2, 1983): 12–14.

Mission Forum (Maryknoll Fathers and Brothers), 8th ser., no. 2 (1979).

Mittler, Barbara. *A Newspaper for China? Power, Identity and Change in Shanghai's News Media, 1872–1912.* Cambridge, MA: Harvard University Asia Center, 2004.

Morrison, G. E. *An Australian in China.* London: Horace Cox, 1895.

Mosher, Steven W. *Broken Earth: The Rural Chinese.* New York: Free Press, 1983.

Mungello, D. E. "The Return of the Jesuits to China in 1841 and the Chinese Christian Backlash." *Sino-Western Cultural Relations Journal* 27 (2005): 9–46.

———. "The Seventeenth-Century Jesuit Translation Project of the Confucian Four Books." In *East Meets West: The Jesuits in China, 1582–1773,* edited by Charles E. Ronan, SJ, and Bonnie B. C. Oh, 252–72. Chicago: Loyola University Press, 1988.

———. *Spirit and the Flesh in Shandong, 1650–1785.* Lanham, MD: Rowman & Littlefield, 2001.

Naquin, Susan, and Evelyn S. Rawski. *Chinese Society in the Eighteenth Century.* New Haven, CT: Yale University Press, 1987.

"Nécrologie. R. P. Gabriel Palatre." *Les Missions Catholiques* (July 25, 1879): 362.

New York Times.

Nicholas Standaert, ed. *Handbook of Christianity in China.* Vol. 1, *635–1800.* Leiden: Brill, 2001.

Nienhauser, William H., Jr. *Indiana Companion to Traditional Chinese Literature.* Bloomington: Indiana University Press, 1986.

Ninü xianbao lu [A description of the punishments inflicted on those who drown little girls]. Nanjing, 1874.

Palatre, Gabriel, SJ. *L'infanticide et l'oeuvre de la Sainte-Enfance en Chine.* Shanghai: Mission catholique à l'orphelinat de Tou-sè-wè, 1878. Includes a seventy-four-page appendix containing sixty-six Chinese documents and six folded leaves of plates.

Pelliot, Paul. "Le voyage de MM. Gabet et Huc à Lhasa." *T'oung Pao* 24 (1926): 133–77.

Pfister, Louis, SJ. *Notices biographiques et bibliographiques sur les Jésuites de l'ancienne mission de Chine, 1552–1773.* Variétés Sinologiques 59. 2 vols. Shanghai: Imprimerie de la Mission Catholique, 1932–1934.

Polo, Marco. *The Travels.* Translated by Roland Latham. London: Penguin, 1958.

Pruitt, Ida. *A Daughter of Han: The Autobiography of a Chinese Working Woman.* New Haven, CT: Yale University Press, 1945.

———. *Old Madam Yin: A Memoir of Peking Life, 1926–1938.* Stanford, CA: Stanford University Press, 1979.

Rawski, Evelyn Sakakida. *Education and Popular Literacy in Ch'ing China.* Ann Arbor: University of Michigan Press, 1979.

Reinders, Eric. *Borrowed Gods and Foreign Bodies.* Berkeley: University of California Press, 2004.

Renaud, Rosario. *Süchow—Diocèse de Chine.* Vol. 1 (1882–1931). Montreal: Éditions Bellarmin, 1955.

Ricci, Matteo. *Fonti Ricciane.* Edited by Pasquale M. D'elia. 3 vols. Rome: Liberia dello Stato, 1942–49.

Riji gushi xuji [The collection of diary stories continued]. N.p., n.d.

Ripa, Matteo. *Memoirs of Father Ripa.* Translated by Fortunato Prandi. London: John Murray, 1844.

———. *Storia della fondazione della Congregazione e del Collegio de'Chinese.* 3 vols. Naples, 1832.

Rose, Lionel. *The Massacre of the Innocents: Infanticide in Britain, 1800–1939.* London: Routledge, 1986.

Rosso, Antonio Sisto, OFM. *Apostolic Legations to China of the Eighteenth Century.* South Pasadena, CA: P. D. & Ione Perkins, 1948.

Sakai, Tadao. "Confucianism and Popular Educational Works." In *Self and Society in Ming Thought,* edited by William Theodore de Bary, 331–66. New York: Columbia University Press, 1970.

Sarcey, Francisque. "Les Petits Chinois." *Le XIXe Siècle* (Paris), November 30–December 19, 1875.

Sauret, Alain. "China's Role in the Foundation and Development of the Pontifical Society of the Holy Childhood." In *Historiography of the Chinese Catholic Church (Nineteenth and Twentieth Centuries),* edited by Jeroom Heyndrickx, CICM, 247–72. Leuven: Ferdinand Verbiest Foundation, K. U. Leuven, 1994.

Servière, J. de la. *Histoire de la mission du Kiang-nan: Jésuites de la province de France (Paris) (1840–1899).* Vols. 1 and 2. Shanghai: Imprimerie de la Mission Catholique, 1914.

Sharping, Thomas. *Birth Control in China, 1949–2000.* London: RoutledgeCurzon, 2003.

Shenbao (Shanghai newspaper).

Smith, Arthur H. *Village Life in China: A Study in Sociology.* New York: Fleming H. Revell, 1899.

Smith, George. *A Narrative of an Exploratory Visit to Each of the Consular Cities of China, and to the Islands of Hong Kong and Chusan, in Behalf of the Church Missionary Society in the Years 1844, 1845, 1846.* London: Seeley, 1847.

Stockard, Janice E. *Marriage Patterns and Economic Strategies in South China, 1860–1930.* Stanford, CA: Stanford University Press, 1989.

Stöcklein, Joseph, ed. *Neue Welt-Bote.* Vols. 1 and 2. Augpurg, Grätz, Austria, 1726–1727.

Sweeten, Alan Richard. *Christianity in Rural China: Conflict and Accommodation in Jiangxi Province, 1860–1900.* Ann Arbor, MI: Center for Chinese Studies, 2001.

Symonds, Deborah A. *Weep Not for Me: Women, Ballads, and Infanticide in Early Modern Scotland.* University Park: Pennsylvania State University Press, 1997.

Taveirne, Patrick. *Han-Mongol Encounters and Missionary Endeavors: A History of Scheut in Ordos (Hetao), 1874–1911.* Leuven: Leuven University Press, 2004.

Terzani, Tiziano. *Behind the Forbidden Door: Travels in Unknown China.* New York: Henry Holt, 1986.

Thomaz de Bossierre, Mme Yves de. *François-Xavier Dentrecolles et l'apport de la Chine à l'Europe du XVIIIe siècle.* Paris: Belles Lettres, 1982.

Thoms, P. P., trans. "Prohibitions Addressed to the Chinese Converts of the Romish Faith." *Chinese Repository* 20 (February 1851): 85–94.

Tiedemann, R. G. "A Necessary Evil: The Contribution of Chinese 'Virgins' to the Growth of the Catholic Church in Late Qing China." Forthcoming.

——. "Not Every Martyr Is a Saint! The Juye Missionary Case of 1897 Reconsidered." In *A Lifelong Dedication to the China Mission: Essays Presented in Honor of Father Jeroom Heyndricks, CICM*, edited by Noël Golvers and Sara Lievens, 589–617. Leuven: Ferdinand Verbiest Institute, K. U. Leuven, 2007.

Van den Brandt, J. *Les Lazaristes en Chine, 1697–1935: Notes Biographiques.* Beijing, 1936.

Verhaeren, H., CM. *Catalogue de la Bibliothèque du Pé-t'ang.* Beijing: Imprimerie des Lazaristes, 1949.

——. "Ordonnances de la Sainte Église." *Monumenta Serica* (Beijing) 4 (1939–1940): 451–77.

Wagner, Rudolf. "The Early Chinese Newspapers and the Chinese Public Sphere." *European Journal of East Asian Studies* 1 (2001): 1–33.

Waley, Arthur, trans. *The Book of Songs.* London: George Allen and Unwin, 1937.

Wall Street Journal.

Waltner, Ann. "Infanticide and Dowry in Ming and Early Qing China." In *Chinese Views of Childhood*, edited by Anne Behnke Kinney, 193–217. Honolulu: University of Hawaii Press, 1995.

Wan Zhaolin. "Quanshan yu jiaohua Qingdai yu zhi de cishan shiye yu jiaohua linian." July 23, 2007. At www.chinasocialpolicy.org.

Wang Yu-jung, Joseph. *Les 120 nouveaux saints martyrs de Chine.* Taiwan: Chinese Regional Bishops' Conference, 2000.

Warren, Leonard. *Adele Marion Fielde: Feminist, Social Activist, Scientist.* London: Routledge, 2002.

Wei Tsing-sing, Louis. *La politique missionnaire de France en Chine, 1842–1856.* Paris: Nouvelles Éditions Latines, 1960.

White, Tyrene. *China's Longest Campaign: Birth Planning in the People's Republic, 1949–2005.* Ithaca, NY: Cornell University Press, 2006.

Whyte, Bob. *Unfinished Encounter: China and Christianity.* London: Collins, 1988.

Wiest, Jean-Paul. *Maryknoll in China: A History, 1918–1955.* Armonk, NY: M. E. Sharpe, 1988.

Williams, C. A. S. *Chinese Symbolism and Art Motifs.* 2nd ed. Rutland, UK: Tuttle, 1974.

Willams, S. Wells. *The Middle Kingdom.* Rev. ed. 2 vols. New York: Charles Scribner's Sons, 1898.

——. Review of *China Opened*, by Charles Gutzlaff. *Chinese Repository* 8, no. 2 (June 1839): 84–98.

Wolf, Arthur P., and Chieh-shan Huang. *Marriage and Adoption in China, 1845–1945.* Stanford, CA: Stanford University Press, 1980.

Wu Ch'eng-en. *The Journey to the West.* Translated by Anthony C. Yu. Chicago: University of Chicago Press, 1977.

Xinbao (Shanghai newspaper).

Xuetang jiangyu [Discourses on morality]. New ed. N.p., 1860.

Xuetang riji [School diary].

Yang, C. K. *Religion in Chinese Society.* Berkeley: University of California Press, 1961.

Yu Zhi. *Deyi lu* [Collection of useful things]. 8 *juan*. Shanghai: Yihuatang Bookshop, 1869. August 22, 2007. At bbs4.xilu.com/cgi-bin/bbs/view?forum=wave 99&message=26812.

———. "Infant Protection Society." Translated by Clara Yu. In *Chinese Society: A Sourcebook*. 2nd ed. Edited by Patricia Buckley Ebrey, 313–17. New York: Free Press, 1993.

Yuyingtang de Douzheng (Shanghai, 1973), n.p.

Zhengying baoying lu [Record of rewards for those who save children]. Reprinted 1869, n.p.

Notes

CHAPTER 1: FEMALE INFANTICIDE

1. Jim Yardley, "Dead Bachelors in Remote China Still Find Wives," *New York Times*, October 5, 2006, A1.

2. *Book of Odes* (*Shijing*), odes (Mao numbers) 245, 300.

3. See Anne Birrell, *Chinese Mythology: An Introduction* (Baltimore: Johns Hopkins University Press, 1999), 116–18; and Anne Behnke Kinney, *Representations of Childhood and Youth in Early China* (Stanford, CA: Stanford University Press, 2004), 111.

4. John Boswell, *The Kindness of Strangers: The Abandonment of Children in Western Europe from Late Antiquity to the Renaissance* (Chicago: University of Chicago Press, 1988), 44, 160, 429.

5. Boswell, *Kindness of Strangers*, 172–79.

6. Benvenuto Cellini, *Autobiography*, trans. George Bull, rev. ed. (London: Penguin, 1998), 335–36.

7. William L. Langer, "Infanticide: A Historical Survey," *History of Childhood Quarterly* 1 (1973): 353–65: 2 (1974): 129–34.

8. Rachel Ginnes Fuchs, *Abandoned Children: Foundlings and Child Welfare in Nineteenth-Century France* (Albany: State University of New York Press, 1984), 5–13, 277.

9. Boswell, *Kindness of Strangers*, 433.

10. David I. Kertzer, *Sacrificed for Honor: Italian Infant Abandonment and the Politics of Reproductive Control* (Boston: Beacon, 1993), 4, 103–10.

11. Langer, "Infanticide," 1 (1973): 356.

12. Kertzer, *Sacrificed for Honor*, 10–13, 16–37.

13. Joseph McDonagh, *Child Murder and British Culture 1720–1900* (Cambridge, UK: Cambridge University Press, 2003), 2–3; Lionel Rose, *The Massacre of the Innocents: Infanticide in Britain 1800–1939* (London: Routledge, 1986), 1–14.

14. Langer, "Infanticide," 1 (1973): 360–61.

15. Fuchs, *Abandoned Children*, 64–66.

16. Arthur Waley, trans., *The Book of Songs* (London: George Allen and Unwin, 1937), 283–84. Cf. James Legge, trans., *The Chinese Classics*, 5 vols. (Oxford: Oxford University Press, 1893), 4: 306–7.

17. *Guanzi*, chap. 16. The *Guanzi* is attributed to Guan Zhong (d. 645 BC), but it was not compiled until around 26 BC by Liu Xiang. See also the entry on *Kuan tzu* by W. Allyn Rickett in *Early Chinese Texts: A Bibliographical Guide*, ed. Michael Loewe (Berkeley: Society for the Study of Early China, 1993), 244.

18. James Z. Lee and Wang Feng, *One Quarter of Humanity: Malthusian Mythology and Chinese Realities* (Cambridge, MA: Harvard University Press, 1999), 177; Kinney, *Representations*, 97–118.

19. H. L. Lowe (Lu Xingyuan), *The Adventures of Wu*, 2 vols. (Beijing: Peking Chronicle, 1940–1941), 1:18–25.

20. James Legge, trans., *Li Chi—Book of Rites*, in *Sacred Books of the East* (Oxford: Oxford University Press, 1885), 27:473–74.

21. Charlotte Furth, "Concepts of Pregnancy, Childbirth, and Infancy in Ch'ing Dynasty China," *Journal of Asian Studies* 46 (1987): 20–21, 25.

22. Lin Yutang, *The Gay Genius: The Life and Times of Su Tungpo* (New York: John Day, 1947), 220–23. Su Dongpo's concern over infanticide is mentioned in Yu Zhi, *Deyi lu* [Collection of useful things], 8 *juan* (Shanghai: Yihuatang Bookshop, 1869), 1:2, reproduced in Gabriel Palatre, SJ, *L'infanticide et l'oeuvre de la Sainte-Enfance en Chine* (Shanghai: Tou-sè-wè, 1878), 86, app. 47.

23. Patricia Buckley Ebrey, *The Inner Quarters* (Berkeley: University of California Press, 1993), 182.

24. Jacques Gernet, *Daily Life in China on the Eve of the Mongol Invasion, 1250–1276*, trans. H. M. Wright (Stanford, CA: Stanford University Press, 1962), 148–49; Marco Polo, *The Travels*, trans. Roland Latham (London: Penguin, 1958), 203.

25. Herbert Giles, organizer, "The Prevalence of Infanticide in China," *Journal of the North China Branch of the Royal Asiatic Society* 20 (1885): 39.

26. Matteo Ricci, *Fonti Ricciane*, ed. Pasquale M. D'elia, 3 vols. (Rome: La Libreria dello Stato, 1942–49), 1:98–99.

27. Gabriel Palatre, *L'infanticide et l'oeuvre de la Sainte-Enfance en Chine* (Shanghai: Mission catholique à l'orphenilat de Tou-sé-wei, 1878), 118.

28. Li Jiugong, *Shensi lu* [Record of careful reflections], in *Yesuhui Luoma danganguan Ming-Qing Tianzhujiao wenxian*, ed. Nicolas Standaert and Adrian Dudink, 12 vols. (Taipei: Ricci Institute, 2002), 9:178.

29. Palatre, *L'infanticide*, 120.

CHAPTER 2: FEMALE INFANTICIDE IN NINETEENTH-CENTURY CHINA

1. "Prohibitions Addressed to Chinese Converts of the Romish Faith," trans. P. P. Thoms, *Chinese Repository* 20 (February 1851): 92.

2. Samuel Couling, *The Encyclopedia Sinica* (Shanghai: Kelly & Walsh, 1917), 249; Bernice J. Lee, "Female Infanticide in China," in *Women in China: Current Directions in Historical Scholarship* (Youngstown, NY: Philo, 1981), 163–64.

3. Monsignor Laribe, vicar apostolic of Jiangxi, December 8, 1845, *Annales de l'Oeuvre de la Sainte-Enfance* 1: (1846–1849): 274, cited in Gabriel Palatre, SJ, *L'infanticide et l'oeuvre de la Sainte-Enfance en Chine* (Shanghai: Mission catholique à l'orphelinat de Tou-sè-wè, 1878), 22.

4. N. B. Dennys, "Shanghai. General Geographical Description, Etc.," in *The Treaty Ports of China and Japan*, ed. William Frederick Mayers, N. B. Dennys, and Charles King (London: Trübner, 1867), 406.

5. Susan Mann, *Precious Records: Women in China's Long Eighteenth Century* (Stanford, CA: Stanford University Press, 1997), 12–13.

6. Susan Mann, "Grooming a Daughter for Marriage: Brides and Wives in the Mid-Ch'ing Period," in *Marriage and Inequality in Chinese Society*, ed. Rubie S. Watson and Patricia Buckley Ebrey (Berkeley: University of California Press, 1991), 204–5.

7. Janice E. Stockard, *Marriage Patterns and Economic Strategies in South China, 1860–1930* (Stanford, CA: Stanford University Press, 1989), 2–3.

8. Arthur P. Wolf and Chieh-shan Huang, *Marriage and Adoption in China, 1845–1945* (Stanford, CA: Stanford University Press, 1980), 1–4.

9. Wolf and Huang, *Marriage and Adoption*, 71, 290, 351.

10. Wolf and Huang, *Marriage and Adoption*, 113.

11. Susan Naquin and Evelyn S. Rawski, *Chinese Society in the Eighteenth Century* (New Haven, CT: Yale University Press, 1987), 107–9.

12. Stockard, *Marriage Patterns*, 3, 70–89.

13. C. K. Yang, *Religion in Chinese Society* (Berkeley: University of California Press, 1961), 47–48.

14. Otto Berkelbach van der Sprenkel, "Genealogical Registers," in *Essays on the Sources for Chinese History*, ed. Donald D. Leslie (Canberra: Australian National University Press, 1973), 83.

15. "Gu shi huiji zongpu" [The collected clan register of the Gu family], Palatre, *L'infanticide*, 89, app. 52.

16. Palatre, *L'infanticide*, 65, 112–13 and Lee and Feng, *One Quarter of Humanity*, 177–78.

17. *Annales de la Propagation de la Foi* 13:453, cited in Palatre, *L'infanticide*, 23–23.

18. Tadao Sakai, "Confucianism and Popular Educational Works," in *Self and Society in Ming Thought*, ed. William Theodore de Bary (New York: Columbia University Press, 1970), 341–45.

19. Kenneth K. S. Ch'en, *Buddhism in China: A Historical Survey* (Princeton, NJ: Princeton University Press, 1964), 13.

20. H. Kern, trans., *Saddharma-Pundarika, or The Lotus of the True Law* (Oxford: Clarendon, 1884), 409.

21. Ho-tong-tse, *Zhengying baoying lu* [Record of rewards for those who save children] (repr. 1869), 5, in Palatre, *L'infanticide*, 61, app. 22.

22. *Guobao tu* [Just rewards illustrated], 9, in Palatre, *L'infanticide*, 74–75, app. 34.

23. *Xuetang riji* [School diary], new ed., 39, in Palatre, *L'infanticide*, 59, app. 20.

24. Maxine Hong Kingston, *The Woman Warrior: Memoirs of a Girlhood among Ghosts* (New York: Knopf, 1977), 86.

25. *Ninü xianbao lu* [A description of the punishments inflicted on those who drown little girls] (Nanjing, 1874), 2, in Palatre, *L'infanticide*, 78, app. 38.

26. Liang-ki-koei [Liang Qigui?], *Xuetang riji* [Diary for schools], Suzhou ed. (1868), 38, in Palatre, *L'infanticide*, 57–58, app. 18.

27. Ho-tong-tse, *Xuetang jiangyu* [Discourses on morality], new. ed. (1860), 19, in Palatre, *L'infanticide*, 52–53, app. 14.

28. Ho-tong-tse, *Zhengying baoying lu*, 1, in Palatre, *L'infanticide*, 62, app. 23.

29. Anne Swann Goodrich, *Chinese Hells* (St. Augustin, Germany: Monumenta Serica, 1981), 71–72.

30. Ho-tong-tse, *Zhengying baoying lu*, 7, in Palatre, *L'infanticide*, 62–63, app. 24.

31. Ho-tong-tse, *Zhengying baoying lu*, 11, in Palatre, *L'infanticide*, 66–67, app. 26.

32. *Guobao tu* [Illustrations of just rewards], one of 4 vols. that compose *Zhuyu yuan* [The round pearl] (Shanghai, n.d.), 8, in Palatre, *L'infanticide*, 74, app. 33.

33. *Guobao tu*, 1, in Palatre, *L'infanticide*, 73–74, app. 32.

34. Ho-tong-tse, *Zhengying baoying lu*, 7, in Palatre, *L'infanticide*, 66, app. 25.

35. *Cihang pudu ce* [Collection of the compassionate ship for passing through the Sea of the World], repr. in Tongzhi reign (1862–1874), 27, in Palatre, *L'infanticide*, 77–78, app. 37.

36. Ho-tong-tse, *Zhengying baoying lu*, 12, in Palatre, *L'infanticide*, 68, app. 27.

37. Ho-tong-tse, *Zhengying baoying lu*, 14, in Palatre, *L'infanticide*, 69, app. 28.

38. *Daojiao dazidian* [Dictionary of the Daoist teaching] (Hangzhou: Zhejiang Guji Chubanshe, 1987), 346; C. A. S. Williams, *Chinese Symbolism and Art Motifs*, 3rd ed. (Rutland, UK: Tuttle, 1974), 207–8.

39. Joseph Edkins, "A Sketch of the Taoist Mythology in Modern Form," *Journal of the North-China Branch of the Royal Asiatic Society* 3 (1859): 313.

40. *Guobao tu*, 2, in Palatre, *L'infanticide*, 75–76, app. 35.

41. *Guobao tu*, 1, in Palatre, *L'infanticide*, 69–70, app. 29.

42. *Guobao tu*, 5, in Palatre, *L'infanticide*, 72–73, app. 31.

43. *Jiuying xinchang* [Saving young girls—new edition], Wuchang ed. (1873), reproduced in Palatre, *L'infanticide*, 148n, app. 65.

44. Liang-ki-koei [Liang Qigui?], *Xuetang riji*, Suzhou ed. (1860), 29, in Palatre, *L'infanticide*, 55–57, app. 17. This story is also found with some variations in *Riji gushi xuji* [The collection of diary stories continued], 28.

45. *Jie ninü wen* [Exhortation against drowning girls], preface, in *An shi deng zhujie* [Commentary on the lamp in the dark house] (Suzhou, 1849), 46, in Palatre, 51–52, app. 13.

46. *Jie ninü tushuo* [An illustrated warning against drowning girls], 8, in Palatre, 80, app. 40.

47. Yu Zhi, *Deyi lu* [Record of useful things], 8 *juan* (Shanghai: Yihuatang Bookshop, 1869), *juan* 1, pt. 2, 1, reproduced in Palatre, *L'infanticide*, 87–88, app. 50.

48. Evelyn Sakakida Rawski, *Education and Popular Literacy in Ch'ing China* (Ann Arbor: University of Michigan Press, 1979), 140.

49. The broadsheets bound in *L'infanticide* were printed from engraved woodblocks that were preserved in the Dejianzhai Library at the Yuanmiaoguan Pagoda in Suzhou. Palatre, *L'infanticide*, 112.

50. Palatre, *L'infanticide*, 105; Rawski, *Education and Popular Literacy*, 115.

51. *Ninü xianbao lu* [A display of punishments inflicted on those who drown little girls], new ed. (Tsou-che-tcheng [near Nanjing]: Toen-jen-tang Bookshop, 1874), 1, in Palatre, *L'infanticide*, 98, app. 39.

52. Goodrich, *Chinese Hells*, 55–56.

53. Compare Palatre, *L'infanticide*, 75–76, app. 35.

54. Palatre, *L'infanticide*, 111.

55. Broadsheet attached to Palatre, *L'infanticide*, 109.

56. Rudolf Wagner, "The Early Chinese Newspapers and the Chinese Public Sphere," *European Journal of East Asian Studies* 1 (2001): 1–4; Roswell S. Britton, *The Chinese Periodical Press, 1800–1912* (Shanghai: Kelly & Walsh, 1933), 63–69.

57. Barbara Mittler, *A Newspaper for China? Power, Identity and Change in Shanghai's News Media, 1872–1912* (Cambridge, MA: Harvard University Asia Center, 2004), 2–6.

58. *Shenbao*, May 18, 1878, in Palatre, *L'infanticide*, 100–101, app. 60.

CHAPTER 3: OFFICIAL AND LITERATI EFFORTS TO COMBAT INFANTICIDE

1. Angela Kiche Leung, "L'accueil des enfants abandonnés dans la Chine du Bas-Yangzi aux XVIIe et XVIIIe siècles," *Études chinoises* 4 (1985): 16–18.

2. Leung, "L'accueil des enfants abandonnés," 18–20.

3. Wu Ch'eng-en, *The Journey to the West*, trans. Anthony C. Yu (Chicago: University of Chicago Press, 1977), 1: 203–5.

4. Leung, "L'accueil des enfants abandonnés," 22–24.

5. Leung, "L'accueil des enfants abandonnés," 25–27.

6. See biographical entries on Jiang Shiquan/Chiang Shih-ch'üan by Tu Lien-che in Arthur Hummel, ed., *Eminent Chinese of the Ch'ing Period* (Washington, DC: U.S. Government Printing Office, 1943), 141–42, and by Yupi Chen in *Indiana Companion to Traditional Chinese Literature*, ed. William H. Nienhauser Jr. (Bloomington: Indiana University Press, 1986), 264–66.

7. Jonathan Chaves, "A Poem on Female Infanticide by Chiang Shih-ch'üan/Jiang Shiquan," *Sino-Western Cultural Relations Journal* 29 (2007): 1–4.

8. The poem by Jiang Shiquan is translated by Jonathan Chaves. The Chinese text appears in the anthology of poems on social problems and natural disasters *Qing shi duo* [The Tocsin-bell of Qing poetry], 2 vols., ed. Zhang Yingchang (Beijing: Zhonghua shuzhu, 1960, 1983), 2: 25–26.

9. Chaves explains that the first two lines draw on imagery from *Shijing*, poem number 189, "Sigan," from the "Xiaoya" section. Here, a king or prince dreams of bears and snakes, and these are interpreted by a diviner as omens of the births of boys and girls respectively. When boys are born, they are to be given jade scepters to play with; girls are to be given *wa*, generally "roof tiles," but interpreted here as referring to (toy) spinning wheels.

10. Chaves notes that the two demons named Aṅgulimālya and Mātaṅga come from Buddhist texts. The first of the two rips the flesh from the bodies of those being tortured in hell, according to the famed narrative of *Mu-lien Saving His Mother*.

11. According to Chaves, Shao and Du were two ideal administrators of the Han dynasty.

12. Dentrecolles to Madame ***, October 19, 1720, in *Lettres édifiantes et curieuses de Chine*, ed. M. L. Aimé-Martin, 4 vols. (Paris: Société du Panthéon littéraire, 1843), 3 (1703): 292–98.

13. Leung, "L'accueil des enfants abandonnés," 30.

14. Leung, "L'accueil des enfants abandonnés," 33.

15. Charlotte Furth, "Concepts of Pregnancy, Childbirth, and Infancy in Ch'ing Dynasty China," *Journal of Asian Studies* 46 (1987): 22.

16. Leung, "L'accueil des enfants abandonnés," 34, 50.

17. Arthur P. Wolf and Chieh-shan Huang, *Marriage and Adoption in China, 1845–1945* (Stanford, CA: Stanford University Press, 1980), 6–9.

18. Jessie G. Lutz, *Mission Dilemmas: Bride Price, Minor Marriage, Concubinage, Infanticide, and Education of Women* (New Haven, CT: Yale Divinity School Library Occasional Publication no. 16, 2002), 14–17.

19. Baudory's letter was copied by Antoine Gaubil in the latter's letter to Monsignor de Nemond, archbishop of Toulouse, November 4, 1722. In Le P. Antoine Gaubil, SJ, *Correspondance de Pékin, 1722–1759*, ed. Renée Simon (Geneva: Librairie Droz, 1970), 28–33, and *Annales de l'Oeuvre de la Sainte-Enfance* 1:129–30, cited in Gabriel Palatre, SJ, *L'infanticide et l'oeuvre de la Sainte-Enfance en Chine* (Shanghai: Mission catholique à l'orphelinat de Tou-sè-wè, 1878), 147.

20. George Smith, *A Narrative of an Exploratory Visit to Each of the Consular Cities of China, and to the Islands of Hong Kong and Chusan, in Behalf of the Church Missionary Society in the Years 1844, 1845, 1846* (London: Seeley, 1847), 61–62.

21. Leung, "L'accueil des enfants abandonnés," 34, 37.

22. Leung, "L'accueil des enfants abandonnés," 45.

23. Angela Ki Che Leung, "Relief Institutions for Children in Nineteenth-Century China," in *Chinese Views of Childhood*, ed. Anne Behnke Kinney (Honolulu: University of Hawaii Press, 1995), 252.

24. Wei Yijie's petition from the *Shilu* [Veritable records] is entitled "Suanzi duotai" [Infanticide by miscarriage], reproduced in Palatre, *L'infanticide*, 3–5, app. 1. On Wei, see Fang Chao-ying's entry in Hummel, *Eminent Chinese*, 849–50.

25. Official circular from Ying Baoshi, 1866, in Palatre, *L'infanticide*, 24–25, app. 7.

26. Monsignor Father Joseph, October 3, 1847, *Annales de l'Oeuvre de la Sainte-Enfance* 2:70–71, quoted in Palatre, *L'infanticide*, 40.

27. Petition of Wu Xingqing, 1815, and imperial edict of Jiaqing, in Yu Zhi, *Deyi lu, juan* 1, pt. 2, 39, reproduced in Palatre, *L'infanticide*, 12–13, app. 4.

28. Ling's proclamation of June 7, 1873, *Annales de l'Oeuvre de la Sainte-Enfance* 27: 269–72, reproduced in Palatre, *L'infanticide*, 39–41.

29. H. L. Lowe [Lu Xingyuan], *The Adventures of Wu*, 2 vols. (Beijing: Peking Chronicle Press, 1940–41), 2:209–10.

30. Governor Cheng's proclamation of Daoguang year 5, month 7, day 1 (1879), in Yu Zhi, *Deyi lu, juan* 1, pt. 2, 16, in Palatre, *L'infanticide*, 15, app. 5.

31. Wan Zhaolin, "Quanshan yu jiaohua Qingdai yu zhi de cishan shiye yu jiaohua linian," July 23, 2007 at www.chinasocialpolicy.org. See also Leung, "Relief Institutions, 253–54.

32. Yu Zhi, "Infant Protection Society," trans. Clara Yu, in *Chinese Society: A Sourcebook*, ed. Patricia Buckley Ebrey, 2nd ed. (New York: Free Press, 1993), 313–17.

33. *Jiangnan tielei tu xin bian* [The misfortunes of Jiangnan with illustrations—new edition] (Suzhou, n.d.), in Palatre, *L'infanticide*, 83–84, app. 44.

34. Wang's proclamation of 1867, in Palatre, *L'infanticide*, 30–32, app. 8.

35. Yang's proclamation of 1875, published in *Huibao* (Shanghai), January 6, 1875, in Palatre, *L'infanticide*, 33–34, app. 9.

36. Leung, "Relief Institutions," 256–57.

37. Petition of Shen Bing, *Huibao*, January 5, 1875, in Palatre, *L'infanticide*, 35–37, app. 10.

38. Paul A. Cohen, *China and Christianity: The Missionary Movement and the Growth of Chinese Anti-Foreignism, 1860–1870* (Cambridge, MA: Harvard University Press, 1963), 229–61.

39. Jean-Pierre Charbonnier, *Christians in China: A.D. 600 to 2000*, trans. M. N. L. Couve de Murville (San Francisco: Ignatius, 2007), 332–33; Samuel Couling, *The Encyclopedia Sinica* (Shanghai: Kelly & Walsh, 1917), 556–57; Tu Lien-che, "Ch'ung-hou," in Hummel, *Eminent Chinese*, 209–10.

40. *Huibao*, November 16, 1874, in Palatre, *L'infanticide*, 92–93, app. 53.

41. Response of Zhang, 1873, reprinted in *Huibao*, January 6, 1875, in Palatre, *L'infanticide*, 38, app. 11.

42. Proclamation of Shen Bing, 1875, in Palatre, *L'infanticide*, 42–43, app. 12.

43. *Huibao*, January 8, 1874, in Palatre, *L'infanticide*, 94, app. 55.

44. *Huibao*, January 8, 1874, in Palatre, *L'infanticide*, 94–95, app. 56.

45. Palatre, *L'infanticide*, 199–200. See also Françoise Lauwaert, *Le meurtre en famille. Parricide et infanticide en Chine (XVIIIe–XIXe siècles)* (Paris: Éditions Odile Jacob, 1999), 260.

46. Ouyang Yong's petition and the consequent edict are published in Yu Zhi, *Deyi lu*, vol. 1, pt. 2, "Regulations of the Infant Protection Society," in Palatre, *L'infanticide*, 39, app. 3.

47. Palatre, *L'infanticide*, 32, app. 8.

48. *Deyi lu*, vol. 1, pt. 2, 34, in Palatre, *L'infanticide*, 88–89, app. 45.

49. *Minbao*, June 13, 1876, in Palatre, *L'infanticide*, 101, app. 61.

50. Petition of Liu Bingzhang to the Daoguang emperor, *Jingbao* [Beijing gazette], February 15, 1877, reprinted in the Shanghai newspaper *Xinbao*, nr, 30 (February 28, 1878), in Palatre, *L'infanticide*, 21–22, app. 6.

51. Leung, "Relief Institutions," 258–59.

CHAPTER 4: INFANTICIDE DENIERS

1. Ida Pruitt, *A Daughter of Han: The Autobiography of a Chinese Working Woman* (New Haven, CT: Yale University Press, 1945).

2. Ida Pruitt, *Old Madam Yin: A Memoir of Peking Life, 1926–1938* (Stanford, CA: Stanford University Press, 1979).

3. Marjorie King, *China's American Daughter: Ida Pruitt (1888–1985)* (Hong Kong, 2006), 50.

4. King, *China's American Daughter*, 28, 52, 70–72.

5. James Z. Lee and Wang Feng, *One Quarter of Humanity: Malthusian Mythology and Chinese Realities* (Cambridge, MA: Harvard University Press, 1999), 7, 28.

6. Michelle King of the University of North Carolina at Chapel Hill and Julia Stone at the Freie Universität Berlin have been engaged in doctoral dissertation research on female infanticide and child abandonment in China.

7. The term *pudu* is part of a common Buddhist expression, *pudu zhongsheng* (to ferry people to the other shore, i.e., rebirth). See Gabriel Palatre, SJ, *L'infanticide et l'oeuvre de la Sainte-Enfance en Chine* (Shanghai: Mission catholique à l'orphelinat de Tou-sè-wè, 1878), v–vi.

8. Deborah A. Symonds, *Weep Not for Me: Women, Ballads, and Infanticide in Early Modern Scotland* (University Park: Pennsylvania State University Press, 1997), 1–9, 69–94.

9. Kenneth Scott Latourette, *A History of Christian Missions* (London: Society for Promoting Christian Knowledge, 1929), 341–43, 464, 560–61.

10. Art. 6, Proclamation on Infanticide, *Chinese Repository* 7 (May 1839): 54–56. Cf. Palatre, *L'infanticide*, 17–19.

11. Art. 2, *Chinese Repository* 9 (June 1840): 78–79.

12. Ping-ti Ho, *Studies on the Population of China, 1368–1953* (Cambridge, MA: Harvard University Press, 1959), 57–58.

13. *The Life and Letters of Samuel Wells Williams, LL.D.: Missionary, Diplomatist, Sinologue*, cited in Eric Reinders, *Borrowed Gods and Foreign Bodies* (Berkeley: University of California Press, 2004), 65–66.

14. S. Wells Williams, art. 2, *Chinese Repository* 8 (June 1939): 95.

15. Herbert Giles, organizer, "The Prevalence of Infanticide in China," *Journal of the North China Branch of the Royal Asiatic Society* 20 (1885): 43, 50.

16. David Abeel, "Notices of Infanticide Collected from the People of Fukien," *Chinese Repository* 12 (January–December 1843): 548.

17. S. Wells Willams, *The Middle Kingdom*, rev. ed., 2 vols. (New York: Charles Scribner's Sons, 1898), 2:239–41.

18. D. J. Macgowan, "Prevalence of Infanticide in China," *China Review* 14 (July 1885–June 1886): 205–8.

19. [E. Chavannes?], "Nécrologie. Charles Piton, 1835–1905," *T'oung Pao*, 2nd ser., 6 (1905): 508–9.

20. Samuel Couling, *The Encyclopedia Sinica* (Shanghai: Kelly & Walsh, 1917), 550.

21. E. J. E. [Ernst Johann Eitel], "Notices of New Books," *China Review* 16 (July 1887–June 1888): 189–90.

22. G. E. Morrison, *An Australian in China* (London, 1895), 2.

23. Morrison, *Australian in China*, 101–2.

24. Morrison, *Australian in China*, 129–31.

25. Sherri Broder, *Tramps, Unfit Mothers, and Neglected Children: Negotiating the Family in Nineteenth-Century Philadelphia* (Philadelphia: University of Pennsylvania Press, 2002), 197.

26. Arthur H. Smith, *Village Life in China: A Study in Sociology* (New York: Fleming H. Revell, 1899), 259.

27. Leonard Warren, *Adele Marion Fielde: Feminist, Social Activist, Scientist* (London: Routledge, 2002), 51–80.

28. Adele M. Fielde, *Pagoda Shadows: Studies from Life in China* (Boston: W. G. Corthell, 1884), 28–38.

CHAPTER 5: THE EUROPEAN CULT OF CHINESE CHILDREN

1. Father [Claude] Gotteland to Father Guidée, December 9, 1846, in *Annales de l'Oeuvre de la Sainte-Enfance* 1 (1846–1849): 419.

2. William V. Bangert, SJ, *A History of the Society of Jesus*, rev. ed. (St. Louis: Institute of Jesuit Sources, 1986), 455.

3. "Rapport par le Docteur Chappet," *Bulletin de la Société de Géographie de Lyon* 5 (1884): 377–91.

4. Herbert Giles, organizer, "The Prevalence of Infanticide in China," *Journal of the North China Branch of the Royal Asiatic Society* 20 (1885): 26.

5. Alain Sauret, "China's Role in the Foundation and Development of the Pontifical Society of the Holy Childhood," in *Historiography of the Chinese Catholic Church (Nineteenth and Twentieth Centuries)*, ed. Jeroom Heyndrickx, CICM (Leuven: Ferdinand Verbiest Foundation, K. U. Leuven, 1994), 255.

6. Francisque Sarcey, "Les Petits Chinois," *Le XIXe Siècle*, November 30, 1875, 2

7. Sauret, "China's Role," 247–72.

8. *Annales de l'Oeuvre de la Sainte-Enfance* 1 (1846–1849).

9. Hans Eberhard Mayer, *The Crusades*, trans. John Gillingham (New York: Oxford University Press, 1972), 203–5.

10. Eric Reinders, *Borrowed Gods and Foreign Bodies* (Berkeley: University of California Press, 2004), 38, 57–66.

11. Reinders, *Borrowed Gods*, 183–84; R. G. Tiedemann, "Not Every Martyr a Saint! The Juye Missionary Case of 1897 Reconsidered," in *A Lifelong Dedication to the China Mission*, ed. Noël Golvers and Sara Lievens (Leuven: Ferdinand Verbiest Institute, K. U. Leuven, 2007), 591n.

12. Joseph Wang Yu-jung, *Les 120 nouveaux saints martyrs de Chine* (Taiwan: Chinese Regional Bishops' Conference, 2000), 25.

13. *Annales de l'Oeuvre de la Sainte-Enfance* 71A (1920): 99.

14. Sauret, "China's Role," 259.

15. Juan González de Mendoza, *Historia de las cosas mas notables, ritos y costumbres, del gran Reyno de China* (Rome, 1585).

16. J. Van den Brandt, *Les Lazaristes en Chine, 1697–1935: Notes Biographiques* (Beijing, 1936), 45.

17. E. Huc, *Souvenirs d'un voyage dans la Tartarie et le Thibet pendant les années 1844, 1845 et 1846*, 2 vols. (Paris, 1850).

18. Simon Leys [Pierre Ryckmans], "Peregrinations and Perplexities of Père Huc," in *The Burning Forest: Essays in Chinese Culture and Politics* (New York: Henry Holt, 1986), 47–55.

19. See Paul Pelliot, "Le voyage de MM. Gabet et Huc à Lhasa," *T'oung Pao* 24 (1926): 133–77.

20. Brandt, *Les Lazaristes*, 40.

21. J. Gabet, *Un mot sur l'infanticide en Chine* (Liège, Belgium: H. Dessain, 1854), v–vi.

22. Bernice J. Lee, "Female Infanticide in China," in *Women in China: Current Directions in Historical Scholarship* (Youngstown, NY: Philo, 1981), 169.

23. E. Huc, *L'empire chinois*, 1857 ed., 2:393–94, cited in Gabriel Palatre, SJ, *L'infanticide et l'oeuvre de la Sainte-Enfance en Chine* (Shanghai: Mission catholique à l'orphelinat de Tou-sè-wè, 1878), iv.

24. D. E. Mungello, "The Return of the Jesuits to China in 1841 and the Chinese Christian Backlash," *Sino-Western Cultural Relations Journal* 27 (2005): 9–46.

25. The Beitang and Xujiahui libraries contained both Chinese and European-language books. For a list of European-language articles on the Beitang Library, see Noël Golvers, "Western Primary Sources," in *Handbook of Christianity in China*, vol. 1, *635–1800*, ed. N. Standaert (Leiden: Brill, 2001), 209–11. The European-language books are listed in H. Verhaeren, CM, *Catalogue de la Bibliothèque du Pét'ang* (Beijing: Imprimerie des Lazaristes, 1949). While the European-language books in the Beitang collection are stored in the National Library of China, Beijing, the whereabouts of the Chinese books are less clear. See Ad Dudink, "The Chinese Christian Books of the Former Beitang Library," *Sino-Western Cultural Relations Journal* 26 (2004): 46–59.

26. Leo F. McGreal, SJ, et al., *Portraits of China* (Shanghai: Tou-se-wei Press, 1936), 63–64.

27. N. B. Dennys, "Shanghai. General Geographical Description, Etc.," in *The Treaty Ports of China and Japan*, ed. William Frederick Mayers, N. B. Dennys, and Charles King (London: Trübner, 1867), 350–413.

28. Dennys, "Shanghai," 406–7.

29. Father Colombel, "Ch. VI. Le Kiang-nan," in *Les missions catholiques françaises au XIX siècle*, ed. Jean-Baptiste Piolet, SJ (Paris: Librarie Armand Colin, 1902), 180.

30. McGreal, *Portraits of China*, 34.

31. Jos Jennes, CICM, *Four Centuries of Catechetics in China*, English trans. Albert Van Lierde, Chinese trans. T'ien Yung-cheng, CICM (Taipei: Tianzhujiao Huaming Shuju, 1976), 174–75.

32. Kenneth Scott Latourette, *A History of Christian Missions* (London: Society for Promoting Christian Knowledge, 1929), 234.

33. Sue Bradshaw, OSF, "Catholic Sisters in China," *Historical Reflections/Réflexions Historiques* 8, no. 3 (1981): 202.

34. Latourette, *History of Christian Missions*, 340–41, 559; Samuel Couling, *The Encyclopedia Sinica* (Shanghai: Kelly & Walsh, 1917), 260. Later, the astronomical observatory was moved from Zikawei to Zosè (Sheshan), near the Church of the Pilgrimage and thirty kilometers from Shanghai. The magnetic observatory was moved to Lu-kia-pang, near the railway station of that name on the Shanghai-Nanjing railway line.

35. Huang Zhiwei, translated (with some errors) into English by Norman Walling, SJ, "Xujiahui Cangshulou" [The Xujiahui (Zi-ka-wei) Library], *Tripod* (July–August 1992): 22–35. The most complete account of the library is found in

Gail King, "The Xujiahui (Zikawei) Library of Shanghai," *Libraries and Culture* 32 (1997): 456–69.

36. For an example of this long-term process, see my "The Seventeenth-Century Jesuit Translation Project of the Confucian Four Books," in *East Meets West: The Jesuits in China, 1582–1773*, ed. Charles E. Ronan, SJ, and Bonnie B. C. Oh (Chicago: Loyola University Press, 1988), 252–72.

37. "Nécrologie. (R. P. Gabriel Palatre)," *Les Missions Catholiques*, July 25, 1879, 362.

38. Rosario Renaud, SJ, *Süchow, Diocèse de Chine*, vol. 1 (1882–1931) (Montreal: Éditions Bellarmin, 1955), 69.

39. Hui Qinglou, "'Deyi lu' banben kao lun" [An investigation into the editions of the *Deyi lu*], *Nankai xuebao (Zhexue shehui kexue ban)* 11 (2006): 126–31.

40. Yu Zhi, *Deyi lu, juan* 1, pt. 2. The Jesuits were also aware of the 16 *juan* edition in which this section constituted *juan* 2. See Palatre, *L'infanticide*, 11.

41. J. de la Servière, SJ, *Histoire de la mission du Kiang-nan: Jésuites de la Province de France (Paris) (1840–1899)*, (Shanghai, 1914), 1: 278.

42. Fang Hao, *Zhongguo Tianzhujiao shi renwu chuan*, 3 vols. (Hong Kong: Gongjiao Renlixue Hui, 1970–1973), 3: 276–78. Pfister's book was posthumously published as *Notices biographiques et bibliographiques sur les Jésuites de l'ancienne mission de Chine, 1552–1773*, 2 vols. (Shanghai: Imprimerie de la Mission Catholique, 1932–34).

43. I am indebted to Michelle King for the suggestion that Pfister might have completed Palatre's *Infanticide*. She is engaged in archival research that may confirm her suggestion.

44. Palatre, *L'infanticide*, 114.

CHAPTER 6: CHRISTIAN MISSION EFFORTS TO AID FOUNDLINGS

1. H. Verhaeren, CM, "Ordonnances de la Sainte Église," *Monumenta Serica* 4 (1939–1940): 471.

2. Gabriel Palatre, SJ, *L'infanticide et l'oeuvre de la Sainte-Enfance en Chine* (Shanghai: Mission catholique à l'orphelinat de Tou-sè-wè, 1878), 152–55, translating from D. Bartoli, *Dell'historia della Compagnia de Giesu: La Cina* (Rome, 1663).

3. Fang Hao, *Zhongguo Tianzhujiao shi renwu chuan* (Hong Kong: Gongjiao Renlixue Hui, 1970–1973), 1: 154–55, 271–73.

4. Palatre, *L'infanticide*, 121.

5. Fang, *Zhongguo Tianzhujiao*, 1: 317–20.

6. Palatre, *L'infanticide*, 155.

7. Palatre, *L'infanticide*, 122.

8. Louis Pfister, SJ, *Notices biographiques et bibliographiques sur les Jésuites de l'ancienne mission de Chine, 1552–1773*, Variétés Sinologiques 59, 2 vols. (Shanghai: Imprimerie de la Mission Catholique, 1932–34), 330; Palatre, *L'infanticide*, 156.

9. Palatre, *L'infanticide*, 162–63.

10. Philippe Couplet, SJ, *Histoire d'une dame chrétienne de la Chine* (Paris, 1688).

11. Nicholas Standaert, ed., *Handbook of Christianity in China*, vol. 1, *635–1800* (Leiden: Brill, 2001), 394, 429; Palatre, *L'infanticide*, 124.

12. Gail King, "Candida Xu and the Growth of Christianity in China in the Seventeenth Century," *Monumenta Serica* 46 (1998): 61.

13. Joseph Prémare to Le Gobien, November 1, 1700, in *Lettres édifiantes et curieuses écrites des missions etrangères par quelques missionnaires de la Compagnie de Jésus*, 34 vols. (Paris: Nicolas Le Clerc, 1702–1776; new ed., ed. M. L. Aimé-Martin, 4 vols. Paris: Société du Panthéon littéraire, 1843), 3: 24–26.

14. *Annales de la Propagation de la Foi* 13: 167, cited in Palatre, *L'infanticide*, 164.

15. Jean-François Foucquet to Duke de la Force, November 26, 1702, in *Lettres édifiantes*, 3 (1843): 69.

16. François Noël, report of 1703, *Der Neue Welt-Bote* (Augpurg, Grätz, Austria, 1726), no. 83, vol. 1, pt. 4, p. 17.

17. Arthur Hummel, ed., *Eminent Chinese of the Ch'ing Period* (Washington, DC: U.S. Government Printing Office, 1943), 692–94.

18. Fang, *Zhongguo Tianzhujiao*, 3:48, 53.

19. Palatre, *L'infanticide*, 132.

20. Letter of Jean-François Gerbillon, Paris, 1705, in *Lettres édifiantes*, 3 (1843): 159.

21. Matteo Ripa, *Storia della fondazione della Congregazione e del Collegio de'Chinese*, (Naples, 1832), 1: 363–64, and *Memoirs of Father Ripa*, trans. Fortunato Prandi (London, 1844), 43–44.

22. Ripa, *Storia*, 1: 365, and *Memoirs*, 44.

23. *Lettres édifiantes*, 3 (1843): 292–298.

24. D. E. Mungello, *Spirit and the Flesh in Shandong, 1650–1785* (Lanham, MD: Rowman & Littlefield, 2001), 143.

25. Antonio Sisto Rosso, OFM, *Apostolic Legations to China of the Eighteenth Century* (South Pasadena, CA: P. D. & Ione Perkins, 1948), 202–11.

26. Palatre, *L'infanticide*, 158.

27. Baudory's letter was copied by Antoine Gaubil in his letter to Monsignor de Nemond, archbishop of Toulouse, November 4, 1722. See Le P. Antoine Gaubil, SJ, *Correspondance de Pékin, 1722–1759*, ed. Renée Simon (Geneva: Librairie Droz, 1970), 28–33.

28. Since a French sou (sol) was a copper coin worth only five centimes (one-twentieth of a franc), twenty-five sous amounted to only one and a quarter French francs, which were equivalent to roughly sixty-two to sixty-three Chinese copper cash.

29. Richard Madsen, *China's Catholics: Tragedy and Hope in an Emerging Civil Society* (Berkeley: University of California Press, 1998), 53–56, 76–106.

30. Jos Jennes, CICM, *Four Centuries of Catechetics in China*, English trans. Albert Van Lierde, Chinese trans. T'ien Yung-cheng, CICM (Taipei: Tianzhujiao Huaming Shuju, 1976), 106–9.

31. Standaert, *Handbook*, 1:472; Pfister, *Notices biographiques*, 2.

32. Jennes, *Four Centuries*, 102–3.

33. Jennes, *Four Centuries*, 105.

34. Robert Entenmann, "Chinese Catholic Clergy and Catechists in Eighteenth-Century Szechuan," in *Actes du VIe Colloque internationale de Sinologie* (Taipei: Ricci Institute, 1995), 403–9; Alan Richard Sweeten, *Christianity in Rural China: Conflict and Accommodation in Jiangxi Province, 1860–1900* (Ann Arbor, MI: Center for Chinese Studies, 2001), 27.

35. Sweeten, *Christianity in Rural China,* 28–29.

36. R. G. Tiedemann, "A Necessary Evil: The Contribution of Chinese 'Virgins' to the Growth of the Catholic Church in Late Qing China" (forthcoming).

37. D. E. Mungello, "The Return of the Jesuits to China in 1841 and the Chinese Christian Backlash," *Sino-Western Cultural Relations Journal* 27 (2005): 36–40.

38. Eugenio Menegon, "Christian Loyalists, Spanish Friars, and Holy Virgins in Fujian during the Ming-Qing Transition," *Monumenta Serica* 51 (2003): 355–57.

39. Jean Charbonnier, *Histoire des Chrétiens de Chine* (Paris, 1992), 215–21.

40. Eugenio Menegon, "Ancestors, Virgins, and Friars: The Localization of Christianity in Late Imperial Mindong (Fujian, China), 1632–1863" (PhD diss., University of California, Berkeley, 2002), 320–27.

41. Arthur H. Smith, *Village Life in China: A Study in Sociology* (New York: Fleming H. Revell, 1899), 287–88.

42. Janice E. Stockard, *Marriage Patterns and Economic Strategies in South China, 1860–1930* (Stanford, CA: Stanford University Press, 1989), 72.

43. Robert E. Entenmann, "Christian Virgins in Eighteenth-Century Sichuan," in *Christianity in China from the Eighteenth Century to the Present,* ed. Daniel H. Bays (Stanford, CA: Stanford University Press, 1996), 180–93.

44. Palatre, *L'infanticide,* 138–39.

45. Palatre, *L'infanticide,* 139–40.

46. Claude Gotteland to Father Guidée of Paris, December 9, 1846, in *Annales de l'Oeuvre de la Sainte-Enfance* 1 (1846–1849): 421.

47. *Annales de la Propagation de la Foi* 16: 335–36, 20:275, cited in Palatre, *L'infanticide,* 147.

48. Louis Wei Tsing-sing, *La politique missionnaire de France en Chine 1842–1856* (Paris: Nouvelles Éditions Latines 1960), 84–86.

49. Mungello, "Return of the Jesuits to China," 28–40.

50. J. de la Servière, SJ, *Histoire de la Mission du Kiang-nan* (Shanghai, 1914), 1: 74, 135–44.

51. Palatre, *L'infanticide,* 59–60.

52. Alain Sauret, "China's Role in the Foundation and Development of the Pontifical Society of the Holy Childhood," in *Historiography of the Chinese Catholic Church (Nineteenth and Twentieth Centuries),* ed. Jeroom Heyndrickx, CICM (Leuven: Ferdinand Verbiest Foundation, K. U. Leuven, 1994), 258.

53. Palatre, *L'infanticide,* 165–70.

54. Palatre, *L'infanticide,* 169, refers to the Congregation of the Immaculate Heart of Mary (CICM) as the Congrégation des Missions-Étrangères de Belgique.

55. Patrick Taveirne, *Han-Mongol Encounters and Missionary Endeavors: A History of Scheut in Ordos (Hetao) 1874–1911* (Leuven: Leuven University Press, 2004), 396–99.

56. Taveirne, *Han-Mongol Encounters,* 393, 402.

57. Kenneth Scott Latourette, *A History of Christian Missions* (London: Society for Promoting Christian Knowledge, 1929), 560.

58. *Yuyingtang de Douzheng* (Shanghai, 1973), cited in Bob Whyte, *Unfinished Encounter: China and Chrisitanity* (London: Collins, 1988), 116–17.

CHAPTER 7: FEMALE INFANTICIDE IN MODERN CHINA

1. Jean-Paul Wiest, *Maryknoll in China: A History, 1918–1955* (Armonk, NY: M. E. Sharpe, 1988), 139–40.

2. Mission Research and Planning Department of the Maryknoll Fathers and Brothers, "Beginning an Era: Maryknoll in China, 1924," *Mission Forum*, 8th ser., no. 2 (1979): 24.

3. Bernice J. Lee, "Female Infanticide in China," in *Women in China: Current Directions in Historical Scholarship* (Youngstown, NY: Philo, 1981), 171.

4. Wiest, *Maryknoll in China*, 143.

5. Thomas Sharping, *Birth Control in China, 1949–2000* (London: Routledge-Curzon, 2003), 296–97.

6. Susan Greenhalgh and Edwin A. Winckler, *Governing China's Population* (Stanford, CA: Stanford University Press, 2005), 222–23.

7. Tiziano Terzani, *Behind the Forbidden Door: Travels in Unknown China* (New York: Henry Holt, 1986), 194.

8. Elizabeth J. Croll, *Endangered Daughters: Discrimination and Development in Asia* (London: Routledge, 2000), 35; Greenhalgh and Winckler, *Governing China's Population*, 226–27.

9. Wallace Turner, "Stanford Ousts Ph.D. Candidate over His Use of Data on China," *New York Times*, February 26, 1983, 7.

10. Fox Butterfield, "Secrecy in a Dismissal by Stanford Fuels Academic Freedom Dispute," *New York Times*, June 7, 1983, A1.

11. Steven W. Mosher, *Broken Earth: The Rural Chinese* (New York: Free Press, 1983), 195, 252.

12. John F. McManus, interview with Steven W. Mosher, *New America* 15, no. 8 (April 12, 1999): 22.

13. Jonathan Mirsky, "The Infanticide Tragedy in China," *Nation* 237, no. 1 (July 2, 1983): 12–14.

14. "The Missing Girls: Some Newborns Seem to Vanish," *New York Times*, April 25, 1993, 12.

15. John S. Aird [John Shields], *Slaughter of the Innocents: Coercive Birth Control in China* (Washington, DC: AEI, 1990), 91–92.

16. Kay Ann Johnson, *Wanting a Daughter, Needing a Son: Abandonment, Adoption, and Orphanage Care in China* (St. Paul, MN: Yeong & Yeong, 2004), 12–15.

17. Tyrene White, *China's Longest Campaign: Birth Planning in the People's Republic, 1949–2005* (Ithaca, NY: Cornell University Press, 2006), 206.

18. Choe Sang-Hun, "South Korea, Where Boys Were Kings, Revalues Its Girls," *New York Times*, December 23, 2007, 1.

19. Kay Johnson et al., "Infant Abandonment and Adoption in China," *Population and Development Review* 24, no. 3 (September 1998): 469–71.

20. Karin Evans, *The Lost Daughters of China* (New York: Penguin, 2000), 27. Cf. Johnson, "Infant Abandonment," 51, 71, 189.

21. Patrick E. Tyler, "In China's Orphanages, a War of Perception," review of *The Dying Rooms*, produced by Kate Blewett [pseud.] and Brian Woods [pseud.], *New York Times*, January 21, 1996, H31.

22. Johnson, "Infant Abandonment," 41–48, 51.

23. Ansley J. Coale and Judith Banister, "Five Decades of Missing Females in China," *Proceedings of the American Philosophical Society* 140, no. 4 (December 1996): 421–50.

24. Sharping, *Birth Control*, 288.

25. Andrew Batson, "China to Continue Birth-Rate Control," *Wall Street Journal*, January 13, 2007, A5.

26. Sharping, *Birth Control*, 292–94.

27. Johnson, "Infant Abandonment," 6–8.

28. "The Sex Ratio: How the Balance Became So Skewed," *New York Times*, July 21, 1993, A6; Coale and Banister, "Five Decades," 445–46.

29. Nicholas D. Kristof, "A Mystery from China's Census: Where Have Young Girls Gone?" *New York Times*, June 17, 1991, A1.

30. Elisabeth Rosenthal, "Bias for Boys Leads to Sale of Baby Girls in China," *New York Times*, July 20, 2003.

31. Jim Yardley, "Dead Bachelors in Remote China Still Find Wives," *New York Times*, May 5, 2006, A1.

32. Evans, *Lost Daughters*, 14–15.

33. Johnson, "Infant Abandonment," 145–49.

34. Geoffrey A. Fowler and Elizabeth Bernstein, "China Weighs Rules Restricting Adoptions," *Wall Street Journal*, December 20, 2006, D1.

35. Johnson, "Infant Abandonment," 135–36.

36. Jim Yardley, "China to Reconsider One-Child Limit, an Official Suggests," *New York Times*, February 29, 2008, A4.

37. Jean Charbonnier, *Histoire des Chrétiens de Chine* (Paris: Desclée/Bégédis, 1992), 506.

38. Nicholas D. Kristof, "Young in China Being Stirred by an Old-Time Christianity," *New York Times*, April 12, 1989, A1.

Index

Page numbers in italics refer to illustrations and maps.

About the Author

D. E. Mungello is professor of history at Baylor University.